It's Not Your Smarts, It's Your Schmooze

Other titles by Ty Freyvogel

Seize the Century! Turnaround Tactics for Success

It's Not Your Smarts, It's Your Schmooze

How to Succeed Without Being Brilliant

Ty Freyvogel

FAST TRACK™
PRESS

Book design by James Simko/JS Design
Cover photograph by Sandy Rochocowicz/Wetzler Studios

ISBN 0-9715439-0-9
Library of Congress Catalog Card Number 2001119565

Printed in the United States of America
Fast Track Press
Cleveland, Ohio
www.FastTrackPress.com

In memory of the greatest schmoozer of all time, my dad Thomas McTighe Freyvogel, Sr. I dedicate this to all those who, like him, have the smarts to schmooze for the better.

Contents

Part Five

Part Six

Foreword

I hate most business books. I'm supposed to eat soup, move cheese and have a clue about a train. I just don't get it. What does this have to do with business?

Business has always been and will always be about exchanging items of value. But being brilliant and knowing your business just isn't enough. Because at its root, business is not about the union of two *companies*; it is about the connection of two *people*.

So when I read *It's Not Your Smarts, It's Your Schmooze*, it felt right. In my mind, I heard that same sound I love to hear when I hit a golf ball just right. Or the sound and feel of a good serve on the tennis court. You just know it's a winner. That's how I feel about Ty's book. I know it's a winner.

Yes, Ty knows his business and is a successful entrepreneur. But he is most successful because he is a master schmoozer. He never stops meeting and greeting and talking and walking. This guy knows everyone. And if he doesn't know you, he will.

I've known Ty Freyvogel a long time. He's as passionate about business as he is about people. Countless times over the years, he's shared the secrets of schmoozing with me. I listened and I learned.

So as I think about my business and why it's thriving, I realize something very important. Schmoozing makes business more enjoyable as it brings me my best customers. Successful business *is* schmoozing.

In this book you'll find practical advice for everyone in any business. I urge you to heed Ty's advice. It works because it's simple, or it may be, it's so simple, it works. In either case, learn and practice what The Schmoozenator preaches. You'll find yourself richer in every way.

Rocky Bleier
Four time Super Bowl Champion and Professional Speaker

PART ONE

Why Schmoozing Wins Over Smarts

You're brilliant. You have the ability to remember vast amounts of data and use it to make a pretty good living. So why are you so often unable to connect a face with the dozens of business cards you find in your pocket after an event? And if you can't remember them, how will they remember you?

Be honest, have you ever thought, "How did that guacamole-brained moron win the account from the gifted and talented class-valedictorian me?" Was it luck? Personality? Strategically-placed spy cams? Chances are they simply knew the secret of connecting with others. They knew how to schmooze.

Here's what I know about you:

- You are successful. How do I know that? Curious minds, historically, belong to the successful. You must be inquisitive to read a book with a title as uncommon as this.
- You could be *more* successful. Lurking around in the back of your brain is the nagging thought that you could achieve more, *but how?* You understand logical process, so what are the steps?
- You *will* be more successful. It's like doing the hokey-pokey: just follow my lead.

Do you believe it when business books claim success to be fast and easy? Of course not, you're too brilliant to fall for that. Sure, I'd like to believe some magic little pill can make me lose twenty pounds by Thursday, but I know weight loss is a slow and sometimes uncomfortable process.

And so it is with schmoozing. Some will adapt to it faster than others. Some will find it uncomfortably personal at first. But, trust me, it is a simple process and can be learned by anyone. Even the brilliant.

I'm awe-struck by my accountant. Every year she prepares a huge package of completed tax forms, each clipped to a stamped and addressed envelope and each topped with a sheet telling me who has to sign what and where and how much of a check to enclose and then to mail it all by when. The detail is over-whelming. My head almost explodes just thinking about it.

After the rush of the tax season this year, she met me at the club for lunch. I never noticed her enter the room; no one did. She moved from the doorway to the table in a carpet-studying scurry. She never made any eye contact with another in the room. She was as invisible as a human could possibly be.

And I was as *visible* as anyone could be. I talked to everyone as I walked through the room; if they were strangers when I entered, they weren't when I left. My meal was delightfully interrupted with handshakes and back slapping as friends passed my table. My accountant shook her head in amazement. She was awe-struck by *me*.

"I just don't understand how you can talk to all these people," she gasped. "You don't even know half of them. How do you do it?"

"I like people," I shrugged. "I want to know more about them. And somewhere along the line, we become friends. Many become clients, too."

"But you can't possibly remember all the people you've met in this restau-rant today!" she exclaimed.

"If you can remember numbers," I said, "you can remember people."

And I told her about the simplicity and efficacy of schmoozing. Schmoozing gets you what you want – whatever you want. Schmoozing pro-duces results without great effort or cost. Everyone you relate to, whether busi-ness or personal or family, benefits from it. She was captivated as I shared the steps she could take to develop her skills as a schmoozer.

Schmoozing is not a way of life. Schmoozing is a way of *living*. It costs nothing yet it's priceless. It's not new, but it is always fresh. It's the stuff of suc-cessful people, people who could be *more* successful, people who *will* be more successful. Just make the first schmooze.

Schmoozing Defined

What is schmoozing? Simply put: schmoozing is the indispensable career and life tool that gives you the connections for success. It's listening to and speaking with others to establish bonds of trust.

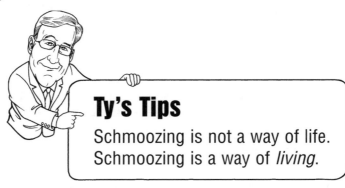

Ty's Tips

Schmoozing is not a way of life.
Schmoozing is a way of *living*.

Does schmoozing sound like manipulative networking? Banish the thought. It shares some techniques, yet networking is geared to the destination; schmoozing is geared to the journey. Networking is an old tired term. Networking is primarily professional but schmoozing incorporates all areas of your life: social, civic, personal as well as business.

Why do most events billed as "networking opportunities" seem phony and contrived? *Because they are.* Schmoozing is real and natural. (Or soon will be for you.) Networking is cold; schmoozing is warm. Networking is calculating; schmoozing is serendipitous. Networking is deadly serious; schmoozing is a great deal of fun.

Here's what schmoozing does for executives, up-and-comers and those who need to kick start a stalled career: It allows them to succeed and then reach greater heights of success. It allows success that is meaningful as well as profitable, and success that is tangible and rewarding.

Schmoozing is both strategy and tactic. It is a business philosophy that fits executives like a hand-tailored suit. Schmoozing is forward-looking. Schmoozing quiets fear and instills confidence. It wears better than canvas and it illuminates better than a full moon in a Pennsylvania cornfield.

For me, the seeds of schmoozing were planted as I watched my father interact in our family's funeral business with those who were grieving. I know it sounds like an odd place to learn schmoozing, yet it was schmoozing in its purest form. By the very nature of the business, it was all about them. It had to meet the needs – both emotional and tangible – of the bereaved. Schmoozing in the funeral business is about the immediate connection, not angling for future business. Asking for referrals would have been awkward, at best.

My dad listened not with his ears, but with his heart. This talent gave him, and then me, the ability to form lifelong bonds with our community. I'm surprised how often my fathers' advice and observations relate to schmoozing. He used to tell me, "Of course there's a right way to do something and a wrong way to do something. Any fool can understand that. But there is also an easy way and a difficult way." Schmoozing is the right way, done easy.

I will admit to having a natural advantage in the schmoozing arena. I came from a large family, married into an even larger family, and then had seven children of my own (my wife, Kathy, helped more than a little). Holiday dinners require entire flocks of roasted turkeys and seating for more than ninety. Having enough family to do a kin-only Hands-Across-America means that when one of us needs an introduction to a prospective company, we usually don't have to look beyond blood relatives. Fortunately for you, the extreme fecundity of the Freyvogels is not a requirement for successful schmoozing.

Schmoozing is the one answer for a thousand difficult business questions and concerns. It is the ingredient most often missing from business plans of all sorts, whether start-up, turnaround, succession or growth.

On one level, schmoozing is practicing The Golden Rule: Do unto others as you would have them do unto you. On another, it's a variation of the *Six Degree* Rule.

To refresh your memory, the Six Degree Rule states that each of us is connected to everyone in the entire world via no more than six connections.

Hard to believe that you're only a half dozen handshakes away from Arnold Schwarzenegger, but perhaps true. Before you begin name-dropping about your relationships with Yogi Berra, Martha Stewart, Mick Jagger and the Queen Mother, remember the Rule says only that you're six handshakes away; it doesn't say a handshake and introduction is imminent. Nor does it in any way suggest they'll become your business customer.

But for schmoozers, it is a reminder that the world, though a big place, isn't really all that big in the end. And that through schmoozing, we can connect with anyone.

Schmoozer 911 Alert

It's time for the Ty Test. If you agree with three or more of the following statements, you are trapped in a business box and doomed to modest success. You have not – cannot – come near your potential. It's a good thing you're consulting with the Chairman of Schmooze.

1. Successful men and women are very smart.

2. I rarely if ever send personal notes to those I consider business contacts.

3. I keep a highly-structured professional and personal life.

4. Most social and quasi-social business events provide no value to my career.

5. I steer clear of discussion of a personal nature.

6. Most of my social engagements are with the friends of my spouse.

7. I do not know if my boss and the person(s) who report to me have children.

8. My stomach lurches when I enter a party filled with strangers.

9. I believe that logic always trumps emotion.

10. Those who smile often are probably stupid.

And lest you think all this connecting is for the soft and meek, even those wearing metal studded leather schmooze. Macho Harley-Davidson created H.O.G. (Harley Owners Group) in 1983 to schmooze owners with rallies and web chats and charity drives.

Have you ever received a chain e-mail? I really dislike these, and dislike these even more when my e-address is dropped in the "To" line with dozens or hundreds of others and visible to who-knows-who all over the world. But I'm amazed at how often I discover people I know hidden several attachments in on the list who appear to have no connection with the e-mail sender.

I was talking with a client in Chicago who lamented that his freelance graphic designer with the memorable name of "Bartholomew" had vanished just when he had a big job to send his way. Two weeks later, I received an e-mailed joke from my son in Italy that had been forwarded dozens of times. Buried in one of the address fields was "bartholomewdesign". Could it be? The Chicago client then tracked the artist down in Winnepeg, Canada.

(For the record: I don't believe that forwarding a chain e-mail to everyone in my data base will change government policy in Timbuktu, and I certainly don't believe that I can make a wish, forward a silly and irritating e-mail to all my friends, and have my wish come true.)

Schmoozing is not a personality contest or a game. It's not the exclusive province of the extroverted or… well, it's not *ex*clusive. In fact, it's just the opposite: it's *in*clusive. Schmoozing works for those who want it to work, period.

Best of all, it's not competitive. It's not a matter of trying to out-schmooze anyone. In fact, when one schmoozer is schmoozed by another, it's wonderful. How could it not be?

CHAPTER ONE

Schmoozing Gets You Where IQ Can't

Trying to succeed without schmoozing is like trying to pick up jelly with a toothpick. You'll have about three seconds of triumph and then, splat.

Your IQ got you everywhere – in school. But now you're in the real world where nobody you know cares if you were class valedictorian and nobody you know cares if you were a National Merit Scholar, if, of course, you know anybody at all. You've got to schmooze to survive. And they don't teach that in school.

Many of the brilliant are in technology fields where job security was high. Not anymore. You can't look to a corporation to take care of you. You have to look out for yourself.

I started in business thirty years ago after a less than stellar college career. As a solid "C" student, I was told my options were limited. Yet I've founded and grown several of my own highly profitable businesses and have a net worth far greater than many of those who had been at the top of the class. And I owe it all to schmoozing.

Brilliance is not required for successful schmoozing. I know, I know, it was your brilliance that got you through school and often lighted your career path. After you are more than a few years out of college, no one cares about GPAs, Phi Beta Kappa keys, or other symbols of brilliance. At this point, it's about your results. Without schmoozing to illuminate your climb, you may be destined to hit a dark plateau.

For schmoozing, brilliance is no more valuable than a flat tire. Let's think about it. Brilliance is often intimidating, which works well for junk-yard dogs and the occasional lawyer, but doesn't inspire others to be part of your team. Being brilliant is not a team sport, but a solitary venture, like being quarantined. Lastly, brilliance is often isolating, valuable to laboratory scientists with attention deficit disorder, but a definite drag in any business with more than one employee.

You will find, as a schmoozer, important information—information that was previously hidden—is easily accessible. And this is knowledge not available on any website. When you need information, someone in your schmoozing network will have the answer. Quickly and easily.

Here's an example, though any accomplished schmoozer could provide you with dozens more. Early on in my career, I had a very solid prospect that was getting hit with a crippling rent increase and felt forced to move his small business out of the area.

Ty's Tips

Trying to succeed without schmoozing is like trying to pick up jelly with a toothpick.

I had spoken with the company's security guard at each visit so I knew he lived in the neighborhood. I asked him what he knew about the state representative there. He told me that the woman representing that area was devoted to the education of children (I wish we had more like her). He didn't know much more.

For me, it was enough. When I called her and told her the problem with the company, that it was moving to an area with substantially lower taxes and taking its employees with it, she was concerned, of course. When I started talking about the effects of lost property taxes on the school system, I could almost hear her sit up straight.

Before the legislature quit for vacation, she had secured assistance for the company which allowed it to remain. It's still there today, by the way, although much larger. And they're still one of my best customers.

The lesson is a simple one. I knew the security guard because I always stopped and chatted with him when I called on the company. But I could never have imagined what a security guard could do for me. Ah, that's schmoozing – you can't tell when the returns will roll in. But you can be sure they will.

CHAPTER TWO

Schmoozing
Swells Income

Twenty years ago I bought a Nutri-system franchise that was $200,000 in the hole. Before you say, "Well this guy must be a bubble left of plumb," you should know that I pocketed around a million and a half dollars from its sale. Not such a dumb idea after all. Schmoozing was the key.

I expanded to the untapped small town markets where good old-fashioned neighborliness is the norm. In a venue like this, you must schmooze or end up tarred and feathered as a no-good carpetbagger. Walmart made its fortune by understanding the importance of the small town schmooze.

I had coffee in the local diners and learned about the residents. Then I schmoozed the homegrown DJs, made them complimentary members of the diet program and got countless hours of free radio publicity as a result. Small town people didn't believe advertising from big city business. But they did trust the recommendations of their family, friends and neighbors.

That same tactic worked magic on an ethnic market in an urban area with my automobile tune-up franchise business. And all the while I was growing my innovative telecommunications business with good old fashioned customer service.

Let me be clear: although I call schmoozing a tactic, I genuinely took an interest in these people. Always a suburban boy in a big city, on the surface it might appear that I had nothing in common with folks in small towns or the inner city. But, at heart, people are the same everywhere. I learned their hopes, their dreams, their joys and their sorrows and I feel honored that I was allowed to share in their lives. When your intentions are truly noble, have faith that the results will be truly rewarding.

As you schmooze, your income increases. There are reasons for it, of course: You know more people and you know them better. Equally important, more people know you and know you better.

Everyone you know or meet needs products and services. In addition, everyone you know or meet offers products and services. Money, like people, goes where it is treated well. And schmoozing is about treating each other well.

I was talking recently about schmoozing results with a friend who is a former closed-minded analytic and now is a very, very accomplished schmoozer. As a direct effect of schmoozing, he found himself making more money than ever and enjoying his family and friends to a degree he never thought possible. "It's nice having the money to go wherever I want," he said with a smile, "and it's even better knowing that wherever I go, I'll have a friend there when I arrive."

You're familiar with Calvin Coolidge's famous observation, "The business of America is business." It's the same with schmoozing. The business of schmoozing is business, too.

If the legitimacy or need for schmoozing in business was ever in doubt, the spectacular crash of the dot com industry made converts of us all.

Dot coms had everything but the most important ingredient: humans. Instant (and temporary) millionaires foolishly believed computers were all that was needed. Computers could answer the phones, computers could do the shipping and receiving, computers could take care of accounts payable and accounts receivable, computers could figure tax strategies, computers could do everything but handle the grill at the company picnic, and rumor had it that R&D was working on a model that could even do that.

The fact is, our lives are made far more convenient, far safer, and far more productive if we properly use machines. But Ford doesn't sell cars because its production line is so smooth. It sells cars because a salesperson talks eyeball-to-eyeball with you, the customer.

It will take some time to figure all the lessons taught with the surge and decline of dot com companies. They were heady, dizzy days followed by confusion and despair. One of the lessons that is clear, however, is the need for humans to interact with humans.

Like anchovies on shredded wheat, schmoozing never fit the dot coms. But schmoozing fits business. It fits business like a hot dog fits a bun, or a sunny Saturday afternoon fits the Pittsburgh Pirates at home.

DON'T STAND IN THE COLD... COME SCHMOOZE!

Because I see the results of schmoozing, I schmooze. It's the same thing with my blood pressure. There's a blood pressure machine at the supermarket here. Every time I go in, I have my blood pressure measured. If it's getting up there, I back off on salt and rich foods. If it's where it's supposed to be, I say a silent prayer of gratitude and make my way to the checkout counter. The point is this: If we see the results of our programs, whether low blood pressure or more profitable business relationships, we're going to continue to improve on that behavior. If we let it, schmoozing generates its own reward.

Schmoozer Hall of Fame

Schmoozer Hall of Famers have a number of common traits. Each has the skill to connect with others in a profound way, each is articulate, and each is wealthy and famous as a result. And each is inquisitive about the world around them and challenges us to be the same.

Jean Nidetch. When Jean first invited friends into her Queens home to discuss losing weight, she just wanted to help others. Her schmoozing turned into the Weight Watchers dynasty. Today, more than 25 million women and men all over the world use Weight Watcher products and services. More than 1 million people schmooze at Weight Watcher meetings every week.

Colin Powell. How can a military man be a schmoozer? Even in this tightly regulated, military society, Mr. Secretary was able to secure the faith and affection of an entire nation and world leaders. He knows that he can best ease or avoid conflict with face-to-face communications, not with missiles. Here's a man who shows us that schmoozing is not frivolous: schmoozing can save lives.

Martha Stewart. Martha has schmoozed her way to the top of an empire of magazines and books, television, radio, web, syndicated newspaper columns, mail-order catalogs, and retail product lines. Through it all she has maintained her schmoozing ideals and stays in touch with those in her Schmooze Zone.

Jack Welch. He was held in such high regard by General Electric's employees and colleagues that they didn't want to let him retire. How, we ask, does the former chief executive officer of a multi-billion dollar, multi-national manufacturing company find himself warmly ensconced in the hearts of his workers, his friends, his stockholders and his neighbors? He's said he believes in driving self-confidence deep into the organization. And without schmoozing, that can't be done.

Oprah Winfrey. Great schmoozers have the ability to schmooze you even over the airwaves. She is a talk show host, magazine publisher, television producer, book club leader and businesswoman. She has millions (both in dollars and in friends) and loves going to work every day. She didn't get that way (and more important, stay that way) by being isolated or greedy or self-centered.

Bill Clinton. When someone can stand behind a lectern in front of a crowd of thousands and make you feel he's speaking directly to you, you know you've found a consummate schmoozer. Politics aside, this guy is good. He has the ability to focus on you and make you feel that your life's concerns are as important as anyone's.

Elizabeth Dole. Maybe it's an extension of southern hospitality. This woman makes you feel like she's waited her whole life to meet you, even if you're simply the banquet manager at the hotel where she is speaking. How? She does her homework to know a little about everyone she expects to meet.

Don Shula. He's interested in the lives of all the famous football players as well as the not-so-famous staff in the restaurants he owns throughout the country. As a waiter told me, "He's just a regular guy who asks me about my family."

Johnny Carson. Few entertainers taught us active listening or schmoozing skills better than he. Solicitous and personable, he laughed with his guests as well as at himself. Every night, he challenged millions of viewers to be as curious as he about all guests, whether famous or not, and about life in general.

CHAPTER THREE

Schmoozing
Feels Good

When I'm really schmoozing, I'm having the most fun I can have without chocolate. I'm on the phone or out in the world, doing what I love most: talking with people. When you schmooze, you never feel like a stranger.

Where once I used to feel a little uncomfortable attending large business events alone, I now know I'll see people I have met through past schmoozing. And I welcome meeting more people who I'll then see at future events. The more I schmooze, the more at ease I am in the world.

Sociologists can pontificate on the human species' need for inclusion in the group for mental and physical health. The simple truth is: Schmoozing feels good.

In our impersonal world of e-mails and faxes and computers, we often feel alienated. Whether by choice or by circumstance, loners may be self-sufficient, but they're usually also unhappy. Take charge and reach out.

I know a very successful business owner. She spends 3-5 days a week on the road, but works very hard at keeping her vast network of family and friends close to her. Even though it is frequently inconvenient, she excuses herself from business every mid-afternoon and calls one or two people for a five minute chat.

"My family and pals keep me grounded," she says. "Some people take a coffee break – I take a friend break."

And when she mentions that she is off to a new city on business and hears, "My husband's old college buddy, John, lives there," she doesn't hesitate to call John and ask him for some restaurant and hotel recommendations. More often than not, the person she has called invites her for a drink or dinner making a lonely business trip less so. And she has received business leads months or even years later from many of these new friends.

Schmoozers are treated well because they treat others well. Makes sense, doesn't it? Yet there are those who find that idea foreign, who believe it's anti-competitive, who think only the weak treat others well. Wrong. And a look at the leaders in Fortune 500 companies proves it.

If you take schmoozing to heart, someday you'll have worthwhile schmoozing advice for me. You'll collect astute observations about men and women, business and pleasure, schmoozing and life. Schmoozing will be just as good, just as faithful and just as rewarding as you are to schmoozing. Will we really meet and talk like that? You never know. That's one of life's best features. You just never know.

Ty's Tips
Brilliance is not required for successful schmoozing.

How to be Smart and Successful

Howard Gardner, Daniel Goleman and decades of research have shown that your ability to handle your emotions and interact well with others is more indicative of success than I.Q. The combination of superior intelligence and emotional health can have a synergistic effect on your career. How do you stack up?

The Traditionally Intelligent

- Your I.Q. is composed only of cognitive skills and factual knowledge.

The Emotionally Intelligent

- You know what you are feeling and use those feelings to make good decisions.

- You manage distressing moods well and control your impulses.

- You remain motivated and optimistic when you have setbacks.

- You are empathetic towards others.

- You have good social skills and get along well with others.

- You manage your emotions in relationships with others.

- You are able to lead and persuade others.

PART TWO

Prepare to Schmooze

Years ago, my wife and kids took a vacation without me. As a home-coming surprise, I thought I'd roast a turkey. How tough could it be? Turkey, stuffing, oven. I'm a reasonably intelligent guy and certainly as funny as Emeril. It would be a piece of cake... er, bird.

I sautéed onion in melted butter, stirred in the bread cubes, rinsed the inside of the bird and patted in the stuffing (without giblets, as my gobbler seemed to have lost his innards).

As I drove from the airport with my family that June, I dreamed about the feast I had created. It had been many many months since Thanksgiving when I last had a whiff of that wonderful turkey and stuffing aroma.

I was beaming as I threw open the door to the house and inhaled deeply. The smells and memories of all that Thanksgiving holds enveloped me: the juicy turkey, the sage and onion stuffing, the burnt, greasy paper... Whoa! Burnt, greasy paper?

Did you know that turkey processors have an odd sense of humor and have been known to hide paper-wrapped giblets inside the bird's neck? Did you know that the smell of that baking paper permeates the turkey and the stuff-ing? (Did you know that it costs $57 to feed pizza to my family of nine?)

I had the best turkey, great stuffing and Food Channel-worthy technique, but without proper preparation the whole meal stunk. And *I* turned out to be the real turkey that day.

My point? I can tell you how to walk the schmoozer walk and talk the schmoozer talk, but it won't help if the inner you, like the stewed turkey guts, ends up fowling up the works.

So step number one: let's take a look at you. We'll scrape out the self-centered, self-defeating anti-schmoozing gray matter and refill that cranium of yours with the stuff of success. Yeah, I know how you brilliant guys hate this kind of introspection, but it's necessary. So keep an open mind – I promise your brains won't fall out.

Ty's Tips

Everything about schmoozers says "open": open for conversation, open for listening, open for friendship, open for business.

CHAPTER FOUR

Break Out of Your Shell to Get Stronger

"Enough of me talking about me, what do *you* think of me?" Hey all you brainiacs out there. I've got news for you. You think too much. Instead of connecting with others, instead of really listening, you're too busy thinking. Thinking of what you're going to say next, thinking of what this person can do for you, thinking of what they think about you. Uh, all this thinking is about... *you!*

Whether it's shyness, greed, social retardation or just general egocentrism, these traits prohibit you from schmoozing's prime thrust: focusing on others. So to be successful, you have to lose it to schmooze it.

Separating the Schmoozers from the Weenies

I went through my early years as shy. Being shy was perfectly acceptable then. There was something endearing about bashful blushing. But I never really thought about the true meaning of the word shy.

Then one day long ago before the magic of spell check, I was looking up the spelling of "Shylock" for a high school report and I saw it right there in black and white. Shy meant timid and lacking in self-confidence. So there was nothing endearing about it. If I was describing myself as shy, I realized I might as well have told the world I was a spineless weenie. And that was the last moment I ever considered myself shy.

As Eleanor Roosevelt said. "Nobody can make you feel inferior without your permission." I no longer handed over that power to others.

While giving a keynote address on the benefits of schmoozing, I met a junior executive named Bob who was skeptical when I told him how valuable he'd be to his office if he were to commit to schmoozing. "Oh, pu-*leeze*" he said. "You're outgoing and that's just you. I'm too shy and that's just me."

Shyness may sound like a reasonable excuse for not excelling, but it's a self-imposed prison. You are so busy thinking what the other person thinks that you don't hear a word they say. What's that old light bulb joke? *"How many psychiatrists does it take to change a light bulb? Only one, but it has to really want to change."* Geez, Bob, just change your light bulb.

If you stop thinking of yourself and your clammy hands and your pounding heart, and become a schmoozer and think of others, I guarantee your palms will dry and your pulse will return to normal. If you fill your brain with thoughts of the needs and desires of others, there won't be any cerebral synapses left for fretting over yourself. When we focus outside of ourselves, shyness means nothing.

A woman I worked with when we were both just out of college told me that once she started schmoozing, her confidence grew. The growing confidence surprised her, she said, because it was so unexpected. When she said that, I told her that the 'schmoozing loop' had been completed. She schmoozed and schmoozed well. She schmoozed without any definite reward in mind. The rewards were forthcoming and nearly tangible, among them, greater confidence. And as a result of greater confidence, she said, she believes she made more money. I have no doubt she's exactly right.

Don't confuse shyness for being soft-spoken. I've known many who barely talk above a whisper, yet are eager to interact with others and have a vast network of business and personal friends.

Lucy has an MBA in finance as well as a dozen years experience. She describes herself as a shy introvert. Friends told her that 'shy introvert' was redundant, but Lucy knew it wasn't. Introverts are not necessarily shy.

She joined the Chamber of Commerce as a way of getting over her shyness. It worked well because along with joining, she was beginning to schmooze, or, as Lucy said, "With schmoozing, the fun you have helps overcome the shyness."

Today she is an active member of two other organizations, the first an investment advisory group for an inner-city hospice and the other a book club. She is still an introvert, but she's not a shy introvert. And she's certainly not a weenie.

The "Act as If" Cure for Shyness

My first business thirty years ago, a telecommunications consulting service, was home-based. A home business was such an odd-ball thing in the early 70s that I hid that fact from clients. And because I worked alone, I felt cut off from others. Somehow in the combination of my isolation and my secretiveness over my locale, my self-confidence started to go down the drain.

BREAK OUT OF YOUR SHELL

One day while feeling worthless after losing a big account, I began to panic over a big sales call I had to make later that day. I felt like such a loser.

How could I possibly close the upcoming deal?

On the way, I stopped at my parish to help with the arrangements for the christening of one of my seven children. As I approached the monsignor's office, I heard him say to someone unseen, "Act as if you have faith, and faith will be given to you." Boom! It was like one of those profound moments in a movie where the hero gets larger on the screen as his surroundings shrink. This was my epiphany. This was the key to my future success. That simple sentence changed my life.

So even though I didn't really feel like a winner, I *acted* like I was the most confident guy in the world. I put back my shoulders, lifted my head, relaxed the worried crease between my eyebrows and strutted down the street to my business appointment.

I boldly greeted the prospective clients, joked and chatted and began to give the best sales presentation of my life. Halfway through, I wondered if I was *really* confident or if I was still just *pretending* to be confident. I couldn't tell. And afterwards as they signed the contract, it struck me that somewhere during the afternoon my confidence had returned full force.

Feeling shy? *Act* as if you are outgoing and you *will* become outgoing. It works. Guaranteed.

"Act as If" Doesn't Mask Greed

I can't explain it, but the "Act as If" principle works on confidence, happiness and other positive goals, but not if your aim is insincerity, greed and deceit. Try to "Act as If" you really care about someone, and they'll always – and I mean always – see through the ruse.

You've probably met at least one Ross in your career. He's the guy who tells you how great you are, laughs at your jokes and pours on the attention. He appears to follow the schmoozing action steps, yet something about his manner is just a little off. He compliments you just a little too often, stands just a little too close, chortles at your jokes that even you have to admit are embarrassingly lame, and manages to find you at every business function and latch on tighter than a skinny flea on a fat dog. Sooner or later, he'll tip his hand and you'll know without a doubt that he's only interested in you for what *you* can do for *him*. And when you realize what this creep has been doing, you'll never do any business with him again.

If you can see through Ross, be confident that the Patricks and the Brittneys and the Matthews and the Lauras will see through you, too. Hey, I'm human. There have been moments when I have been listening to a prospect and thought, "Blah, blah, blah. Let's just get to the part where you sign the contract," while I tried to look like I was still rapt by her banter. But here's what happens: within an instant of this thought, the prospect begins to disengage from me. Not in a big way. Just a little. But enough to jeopardize the sale. That's when my alter ego, Tiny Ty, shouts in my brain, "You big fool! Do you want this account? Then stop thinking about the *account* and start thinking about the account*holder*." And then I mentally shove the evil "g'me g'mes" out of my thoughts. Mark my words: People eventually discover emotional deception. The force won't be with you, Obi Wan, if you go to the dark side.

CHAPTER FIVE

Focus on Others and Connect More

A great schmoozer once told me, "Whether I am with one or many, at a business luncheon or a sports banquet, at my office or at my home, I always act as a host and not a guest. That means putting the desires of others before my own."

Just a reminder of the basis of schmoozing: it's about focusing on *them*. And you can't focus on *them* until you stop thinking about yourself. Now that you've quieted some of the inner noise so you can hear others, do you have any real interest in asking any questions?

The funniest human being I know is a saleswoman named Julie. When she starts in on one of her comedy routines, I hoot so hard my nose runs. She's always the center of attention. People love to be entertained by her. But few *buy* from her. And she can't understand why.

"I work so hard to make people laugh, Guy," she says while waving to people she doesn't know who've entered the room. "I want people to like and remember me." Don't we all? (And the name is *"Ty"*, Julie.) Having people like *you* is not as important to schmoozing as you showing that you truly like *them*. She is so focused on being the life of the party that she makes no effort to learn about anyone else or to make them memorable to her. She needs to work harder on becoming more interest*ed* than interest*ing*.

Forget what you hear cabbies bellow out the window when someone cuts them off – people aren't dumb. They know when you don't really care about them. Julie's "audience" knows on some level that her primary interest is in getting emotional approval. Therein lies her problem closing business deals. People want to know, in your thought, word and deed, that you like them.

Although I do believe we should all love our neighbor, it's hard to *like* him if you don't *know* him. And the only way to know is to ask. A perfunctory, "How are you?" when introduced and then tuning out is not the definition of focusing on others.

Inquiring Minds Want to Know

If you're going to have any success with schmoozing, you have to be inquisitive. The good news: brilliant people are usually curious. Your eye catches an intriguing bit of information buried deep in the Wall Street Journal and you'll spend the next hour on line researching its ramifications. Yes, you can be insatiably inquisitive – about facts and figures and things. The bad news: the thought of questioning a fellow human being about his or her life makes you assume, "that's none of my business." The bad bad news: the thought of questioning a fellow human being about his or her life makes you anxious you'll be asked to volunteer information about your life. All that is bad bad bad news for schmoozing.

If you think it would be utterly inappropriate for someone to ask you if you had children or played tennis or where you went to college, then it's highly unlikely that you would ever ask those questions of another. And if you don't interact with others on that level you cannot schmooze. And if you don't schmooze, you lose.

Why would you be so concerned about someone knowing anything of your life unless you've got something really nasty to hide, such as all those years you spent as a Mafia hitman or undercover with the CIA? (And remember, even G. Gordon Liddy and Jimmy "The Weasel" Fratianne wrote tell-all books.)

I'll tell you why: fear. You're afraid you'll be judged negatively or the information will be used to harm you. Without any real danger present, being overly private is an issue of low self-esteem. Your attention, please: Playing your cards pressed so tightly against your chest is, as shyness is, for weenies. Get over it. Those with confidence have no apprehension of, and in fact enjoy, talking about their lives – all of their lives, business and family included.

Let's be clear: I'm not talking about being indiscreet. I'm referring to the casual interplay of tidbits that most people discuss freely. No one in polite society really wants to hear intimate, behind-closed-doors kind of information. If anyone asks you, as they asked Bill Clinton, if you wear boxers or briefs, you have every right to say, "none of your bees wax" or words to that effect. (And I always wondered why he didn't respond indignantly, "How dare you ask that of the President of the United States of America?") Schmoozing is not about being nosy, intrusive or offensive.

Ty's Tips
Act as if you have confidence, and confidence will be given to you.

But inquisitiveness about others is vital to schmoozing. We satisfy our curiosity about others in lots of ways. Sometimes we listen, sometimes we observe, sometimes we read, and sometimes we ask. And when we allow our curiosity full rein, we enrich our lives.

You know a great deal about your company and the history of your company. You should know a great deal about the market you serve and you should know a great deal about your competition. Now what about your employees? What about your coworkers? If your business is business, then you know the more you know, the better executive you are.

Kick Starting Your Awareness

Earlier, I suggested that many of you might be naturally inquisitive – at least about things, if not people. But what if you are completely indifferent about learning? What if wearing blinders defines your comfort zone? What if you took to heart the phrase, "Curiosity killed the cat?"

Well unless you've recently coughed up a hairball, it won't pose any real hazard if you expand your mind by exploring a new subject. But what? How? If you have devoted yourself to a single endeavor, over the years your world can become very small indeed. So before we throw you into the uncharted water of developing your curiosity about people, let's start by revving up your general inquisitiveness about the world at large.

There's a fine line between the comfort of a routine and the inflexibility of a rut.

Have you ever realized a dream? After I made my first million using the same schmoozing techniques in this book, I did just that. I took a year off with the express purpose of taking lessons from the best golf pros in the country and mastering the game. It all began because I was curious.

I didn't grow up playing golf. In the early days of my career, when my wife and I were creating a large family and I was working hard to feed all those mouths, it appeared golf and I would go our separate ways. But as I rocked a baby, I would watch Tom Watson or Ben Crenshaw or Nancy Lopez and shout at the TV, "How the heck do you do that?" I watched and learned. I did a lot of rocking with my seven babies over the years, and I did a lot of watching and learning. And a lot of shouting at the TV.

Many lessons and many hours of practice and hundreds of rounds of golf later, I have some idea how they do it. I can't do it as easily or as consistently as my golf heroes, or I'd have a better than 12 handicap to show for it. I'd also be on the links instead of running my several businesses, speaking professionally and writing this book. But at least I have the satisfaction of knowing: How the heck do they do that?

The joy I have knowing an answer pales in the thrill of learning the answer in the first place. That wonderful scenario has been played out again and again in my life, in businesses I knew nothing about, but about which I asked, "How the heck do they do that?" My curiosity and love of learning is what has led me to create and turnaround more than a dozen small and million-dollar enterprises.

The question is not important, but asking the question is vital. Over the last decade or so, I've known people who have asked, figuratively or literally, variations on the "How do you …" question. It's a great start to get others talking about their passions, learn a new subject yourself, and build a bond with your tutor. My curiosity leads me to ask everyone questions. And I encourage my fellow schmoozers to ask and learn.

"How do you differentiate the composers?" a friend asked about the symphony. Many orchestras, including the one here, have pre-concert lectures where curious people learn about the composer and the many influences on the music. My friend is today a Chopin aficionado. He's made many friends and received much pleasure from classical music, an art form he previously thought to be baffling.

FOCUS ON OTHERS

"Why don't you get stung?" was the question put to a beekeeper here and his answer was, "Sometimes I do, but when I do, it's because I wasn't careful." That conversation led to a summer job for a neighbor's daughter who today is halfway through her studies for a degree in entomology.

I met a schmoozer on one of my daughter's field trips. My daughter's friend said she made a decision to let loose her curiosity after she realized how she was cutting herself off from learning by not asking the great, one-syllable question every child knows: Why?

She was on a train from Baltimore to Washington and sat with a county coroner. She was fascinated with his job and when she learned of some of the major homicides the coroner had worked on, she couldn't stop asking question after question after question.

"Every so often I would apologize for asking so many questions, but I would add how fascinating I found his work, and he would smile and tell me he was happy to have the opportunity to talk with someone who was this interested."

As a result of her new appreciation for her own curiosity, she later learned why the Japanese economy took such a beating, why the price of gasoline rose faster than the sun, why test scores have little to do with performance and why the Cleveland Indians haven't won the World Series since 1948 (it has lots to do with trading away Rocky Colavito.) Along the way, she met and created relationships with dozens of new people.

When someone suggested that preparation wasn't needed for off the cuff speaking, Winston Churchill replied, "I have been preparing for impromptu speaking all my life." Inquisitiveness gives you some meat to make the good schmoozing sandwich. You have to be prepared for good conversation and that has its roots in knowing something about many topics.

And that's the beauty of being inquisitive. It brings you closer to people, to facts, and to yourself.

CHAPTER SIX

Create a Winning Aura for Easy Schmoozing

If there are accomplished schmoozers in your life, it's challenging keeping all their acquaintances sorted out. People talk to you wherever you go. People talk to you in the elevator, people talk to you in the parking garage, people talk to you in stores and people even talk to you in restrooms. Schmoozemasters send out a signal that says "talk to me".

When I move through this world, I do it with my head high, a confident stride and a smile on my face. I make a point to look at people in the eye as I pass. Everything about me says "open": open for conversation, open for listening, open for friendship, open for business. I say hello to total strangers. I *want* people to talk to me and I want to talk to them. I am approachable and people approach me.

If strangers don't speak to you throughout the course of your day, I truly believe it's because, deep down, you don't want them to. On occasion, when I'm ill or distracted I notice my human tractor beam seems to be on the fritz. It's as if I create a black hole and no energy can leave me to spark others, so no one is drawn to me. Are you putting out a welcome mat or a beware of the dog sign? Do you walk with your head down, your arms crossed and rarely make eye contact with others? Create a winning aura of warmth, and the world will approach you like moths to flame.

Now here's a wonderful, but spooky, benefit to projecting a winning aura. I can't explain it, but my demeanor and attitude draw those *specific* types of people to me that I need in my life at any given time. I left the house one morning knowing I needed to find a web designer and host. An hour later a man struck up a conversation with me while I was standing in a hardware store: he was a web designer and host. I found the editor of my first book in much the same manner. This happens far too often for me to attribute it to coincidence.

The Positive Attitude Puzzle Piece

A big part of your ability to project a winning persona is based on your attitude. If you're truly brilliant, right about now you're thinking, "My *attitude*? What does my attitude have to do with anything? I don't give a rat's rear end about my freaking attitude!"

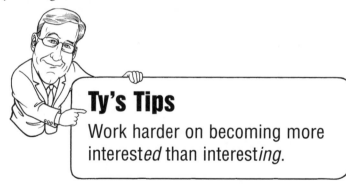

Ty's Tips

Work harder on becoming more interest*ed* than interest*ing*.

A positive attitude is more important than you might believe. It can equal more income just as surely as planting tomato seed produces tomatoes.

Simple? Yes. Easy? No. True? Absolutely.

Attitude is one of the hidden generators of income. C'mon, stop rolling your eyeballs around in your head. I know that suggesting you change your outlook on life seems a bit too warm and fuzzy for the boardroom, but just stay with me.

Let's go over it one more time just to be sure you understand what I'm saying: You create and enjoy a happier attitude and your income will rise. Period.

When I first broached this subject of a happier attitude, a pessimistic friend I was talking with said, "Whaddayou want me to be, the Dalai Lama? I'm underpaid and overworked, I'm saddled with a boss who only smiles when he sees someone trip, and my career has all the fuel of a pop bottle rocket left out in the rain. My attitude is the last thing I worry about."

He was right. Under those circumstances or any combination of them, attitude is the last, and I do mean last, thing we worry about. There's the problem; it should be *first.* The care and feeding of our attitude should be more important than the paycheck, more important than the boss or the career. Attitude should be first because attitude is going to lift you out of your career pit.

Before we talk about what attitude is, maybe we should talk about what attitude isn't. Attitude isn't a pair of shoes you select in the morning, or a restaurant you go to on Fridays. It isn't something you can put on and take off, something you can accept or pass by.

Your attitude is your perspective; it's the focus knob on your vision. Attitude is part of you, just like your blood type and your voice and your signature. As a matter of fact, maybe reminding ourselves that our attitude *is* part of our signature would make it easier to understand the value of it.

Attitude is the way you react to competition, the way you see the value in a team, the tack you take when all the cards have yet to be played.

My father-in-law Jack said it best, I think. He said, "Attitude? A good attitude is like standing on your toes. You see lots that you couldn't see before."

There are behaviors you can now develop that will go a long ways toward your schmoozer education. As these behaviors become second nature, the flow of income, both personal and professional, will continue to increase. You may not find schmoozing in your comfort zone. But push yourself to new ground. You'll grow stronger every time you do.

I once knew a steel company executive about whom it was often said, "Even his friends don't like him." Little wonder. Self-absorbed, materialistic, stingy. But an accomplished executive in the tumultuous steel industry. And then the steel mill went bankrupt. Well it was schmooze or lose, so he gave the process a major test. Schmoozing was not easy for him. But he stuck with it and just accepted an offer to join a young manufacturing company. He is making more money than ever. And amazingly, the people he thinks of as friends think of him as a friend, too.

A friend who has had great success as a schmoozer told me this and I'll never forget it. "I took to schmoozing," he said, "like kids take to candy. And I was enjoying myself as I discovered my extended family and then beyond that to people I used to know, such as former classmates and fraternity brothers and kids from the old neighborhood. It was going very well when I discovered what I now call 'icing on the cake.' Know what it was?"

He was laughing softly, almost embarrassed at what he discovered through schmoozing.

"I like them. I mean I really like them. Almost every one of them. They're a great group of people. What I thought would be a chore has turned into great pleasure." That's schmoozing for you.

I've shared with you the importance of losing the mental barriers of shyness, greed, pessimism and self-centeredness that prevent us from effectively focusing on others and schmoozing. You've learned how to break out of your shell to get stronger, how to focus on others to connect more and how to create a winning aura for easy schmoozing. Congratulations! You've completed your pre-work and now you're ready to learn the tricks of the schmooze trade.

The Schmoozer's Oath

I swear to fulfill, to the best of my ability and judgment, this covenant:

I will treat others as I wish to be treated.

I will respect the hard-won interpersonal gains of those schmoozers in whose steps I walk, and gladly share such knowledge as is mine with those who are to follow.

I will apply, for the benefit of deficient schmoozers, all measures which are required, avoiding those twin traps of greed and networking.

I will remember that there is art to schmoozing as well a genuine interest in others, and that warmth, sympathy, and understanding may outweigh the need for immediate gratification.

I will respect the privacy of my fellow schmoozers, for their confidences are not disclosed to me for the world to know.

I will expect no thanks. The responsibility to help others must be faced with great humbleness.

I will encourage listening whenever I can, for listening is preferable to speaking incessantly.

If I do not violate this oath, may I enjoy life and art, be respected while I live and remembered with affection thereafter. May I always act so as to preserve this finest of traditions and may I long experience the joy of schmoozing.

PART THREE

Schmooze Dos

"Don't you like your dessert?" the man next to me at a business association luncheon asked as I pushed away the strawberry pie.

"I hate strawberries," I shrugged.

"Hate *strawberries*? You're kidding! Who could possibly hate strawberries?" he retorted in disbelief and looked at me as if I had suggested I hate Mom, apple pie and the American flag. "I *love* strawberries! They're my favorite fruit. I slice them on my cereal every day and often have an evening snack of a strawberry smoothie." He then told me more than any human being should know about strawberries and how he thought they were the wonder food.

Two weeks later he called me at the office. "Hey, good buddy. It's George."

"George!" I repeated with great schmoozer warmth as I rapidly searched my memory banks. *George, who?*

"George Gold from Discount Office Products," he continued, sensing I didn't remember him. "We had that great conversation at the business luncheon. Remember?"

No, George, I do not remember you. I do not remember you because we did not connect. And we did not connect because we did not have a *conversation*, great or otherwise.

Somehow in our disenfranchised modern lives, we've made 'talking' synonymous with 'conversation'. It is not. Genuine conversation cannot occur until you and another establish common ground.

What *you* had that day, George, was like an eruption of gray-matter lava from Vesuvius. I was superfluous to your aggressive recitation of self-validating preconceived opinions. There was no common ground, therefore no conversation. No conversation, no connection. No connection, no recollection.

Toddlers under age 2 go through a stage called 'parallel play'. Believing they are the center of their own universe, they play *next to* — but not *with* — each other.

And so it is with much of what purports to be conversation these days. Each person regurgitates his or her absolutely-positively must-be-true morsels where they lay unnoticed on the table. This monologue provides only meager nourishment for the lecturer and nothing for the listener. We've been speaking alongside — but not with — others for too long.

Seeking that common ground is vital to your success as a schmoozer. The questions you ask others are merely a tool to find that shared perception – that topic upon which you can develop a dialogue.

Don't misunderstand, we've been *communicating*, alright. George freely communicated his thoughts on strawberries. But communication is just a serve over the net; conversation is the volley.

Let's go back to my certainly-not-good-buddy George. When I said "I hate strawberries," George could have developed his one-sided communication into a conversation in a number of ways. Let's look at one:

"Which dessert is your favorite, Ty?" *(The serve.)*

"Hot fudge sundae. How about you, George?" *(The return.)*

"Strawberry short cake with a scoop of vanilla. It seems like we both like ice cream. Who has the best ice cream?" *(The volley.)*

CHAPTER SEVEN

Hello?
Can you hear me?

Did you participate in debate in school? It's a verbal sport. Debaters take a pro and con approach to a topic and make points and counterpoints. A good debate is an exhilarating contest in which to participate and interesting to hear. But a debate is not a conversation. A debate is competitive.

Schmoozing is viewing others as *collaborators*, not competitors. Collaborators strive to find similarities with which to converse. Competitors focus on differences.

Superficially, the common ground we seek may appear to be subjects (sports, movies, reading) but what we're really doing is using those interests to assess the other's core values. Without a similar value system, trust is impossible. And without trust, schmoozing gets stymied.

An old saying reads: God gave you two ears and one mouth; use them in that ratio.

How does conversation start? It starts with not talking.

"...and that's why my daughter deserves a second chance," I explained to Sister Connie after a minor rule infraction at school.

"I hear you, Mr. Freyvogel," Sister said, and then went on to convince me that she had not heard at all.

I hear you. That expression bugs me like a loud cricket on a quiet night. People who really listen never need to try to convince the speaker with this trite phrase.

What is listening? Is it synonymous with hearing? Not really.

Hearing is what goes on in your brain, body and emotions when you encounter auditory stimuli. Listening is better described as attending another's conversation

Hearing is a multi-stage process, primarily involuntary, that goes beyond auditory reception. When you hear, you get the I.D.E.A.: Input, Decode, Evaluate, Answer. And all steps, except for a portion of the last, are performed subconsciously.

The first stage is Input, or what arrives at your eardrums. We can't truly turn off our hearing. Our ears are working – inputting — 24 hours a day, whether or not we decode the sound. Decoding is the ability to make sense of the words, to translate the words into meaning. I can certainly hear someone speaking Aleutian, but I cannot understand or decode its meaning. Once I've decoded the words, I evaluate or form an opinion about the message. Finally, I answer. Responses or answers are multi-sensory: emotional, intellectual, physical and only sometimes audible. Hearing always elicits a response even if a word is never uttered in return. Here is an example:

1. **I**nput ("The sewer has backed up.")
2. **D**ecode: (*waste... returned... floor*)
3. **E**valuate: (*I do not like*)
4. **A**nswer: Revulsion (emotion), much work to clean up (intellectual), throat tightens (physical), and "I'll get the boots and the mops" (audible).

This is more than just academic mumbo-jumbo. It's important to understand these stages to learn where you as a communicator can avoid snags that can occur in your conversations with others. Here are some tips to help others hear you better.

To insure they are receiving auditory input, make sure the room is not too noisy or distracting. And speak up! The volume required to propel your voice the six inches from your mouth to your ear is far less that the decibels needed to reach the listener six feet away. Always be cautious of cell phones. The signal may seem crystal clear to you but the listener may hear dead air.

The listener's ability to decode or understand your speech is where many problems lie. Your only tactic to assist in the decoding process is by making the message as universally-understood as possible. If you have poor diction and mumble, your message can become distorted. (Do you remember playing "Telephone" as a child?) Likewise, accents, both foreign and regional, can wreak havoc on communication. Seek a voice coach. (Even I'm working on this: I answer the phone, 'yella' in true Pittsburgh-ese fashion.) Finally, sophisticated terminology and esoteric jargon – what my mother called ten cent words – can prove to be as impossible for many to decode as an unknown foreign language. I don't think I'm the only one who has sat clueless in a meeting with a vacant expression as the computer experts' spouted alien cyberspeak. (Yes, the surveys say the listener thinks you're smart when you use "big" words. But the surveys also say the listener isn't able to retain your message!) Use common language.

You have most control over the listener's input, and through thought and preparation may avoid many decoding problems. But bad news, fellow schmoozers. Once you're at the last two steps in the listening process, you're a rider on a runaway train.

Now, subconsciously, your listener will fire up all his or her synapses and evaluate your statement or question. He or she will then involuntarily answer/respond emotionally (joy, sadness, fear), intellectually (cognitive thought about subject), and physically (dilated pupils, rapid heartbeat, increased respiration).

The only voluntary action of the entire hearing process is the last: the audible response. Since conversation is sequential and not simultaneous, to allow your listener to participate in the conversation requires you to… *be quiet!*

Let's spin the spotlight. Whereas before you were exploring how you could make the hearing process easier for your listener, now let's explore how you can encourage conversation by becoming a better listener yourself.

Hearing is mostly unconscious and passive. Effective listening is a consciously-performed skill making use of your mind, body and emotions. And for some, it takes real *work* to be a good listener.

I know this all too well. Listening is something I have struggled with all my life. I have a quick mind; too quick, perhaps, as my mind wanders if someone is a sluggish speaker or unfolds their point too slowly. Some of the following steps are easy for me, but others I have to consciously practice every day.

Eye contact. In this culture, mutual eye contact of three seconds is the norm. Less can be perceived as a sign of deceit, more as aggressive. The word "mutual" is the key. The person speaking may often look away to collect their thoughts. You, however, must look at them, even when they are not returning your gaze.

Facial expressions. Look for the emotion behind the words and use appropriate expressions. You're generally safe mirroring the demeanor of the speaker, but not always. Some people remain deadpan when telling a joke, and others smile to relieve tension when relating tragic events.

Stop distracting habits. Do you have ants in your pants? A speaker feels that people who fidget in their seats, fiddle with pens, tap fingers, yawn and other distractions are bored and not listening. This behavior can derail a speaker's train of thought and cause embarrassment and hurt feelings. (Attorneys in courtrooms have been known to yawn and fuss with paper to draw the jury's attention away from the opposing counsel's summation.)

Stay focused. Don't open up the menu, call to the waiter, read reports on your desk or just gaze at others walking past. No matter how innocent your intent, these actions say to the speaker: 'You and what you are saying is not important to me.' You won't really be believed if you say, "Oh, just go on talking. I'm still listening."

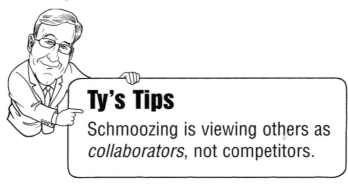

Ty's Tips

Schmoozing is viewing others as *collaborators*, not competitors.

Be patient. Yeah, yeah, yeah. We know you're brilliant. But don't be so quick to finish people's sentences or interrupt. Wait your turn.

Stay engaged. Sometimes we are so intent on thinking of what to say next that we don't hear what is being said. Concentrate. Is it worse to have to take a minute to think of a response, or worse to hear, "Well? What do you think of that?" and realize that you have no idea what "that" is.

Attention noises. These are the umms and uh-huhs and ohs that you softly interject to signal the speaker that you are attending. On the phone, the lack of attention noises can make a speaker repeatedly ask, "Are you still there?" In person, the speaker will begin to feel that you are bored. Be careful, though. Going overboard on attention noises can have opposite the desired effect. Too many uh-huhs will make the speaker feel you are rushing him, and are waiting to pounce with your own comment. Over umm-ing can also sound insincere. As I relayed my medical history to a doctor's office receptionist, she knitted her brows and sadly umm-hmmed at every other word I spoke: "And then when I hurt *(umm-hmm)* my foot *(umm-hmm)* it twisted *(umm-hmm)* my knee *(umm-hmm)*" It sounded like she was purring.

Improving Listening Skills

1. Hold eye contact.

2. Mirror facial expressions.

3. Stop distracting habits. Don't fidget.

4. Stay focused. Don't be distracted by other things.

5. Be patient. Don't finish people's sentences or interrupt.

6. Stay engaged. Don't worry about what you will say next.

7. Make attention noises. Add ums and ahs at appropriate times.

8. Add attention movements. Nod, lean in, touch an arm.

9. Ask related questions.

Attention movements. These include an encouraging or approving nod, a head shake to signify disapproval or disbelief, a tilt of your head to show interest.

And finally, when it is your turn to speak again, briefly answer any questions that were posed (no filibustering), and then ask an open-ended question that cannot be answered with yes or no, and that *relates to the topic on the floor.*

A question relating to the topic is the trickiest part about conversation. If you listen by the book: maintain eye contact, focus in on them, make appropriate attention noises, and then ask an unrelated question, the speaker will believe you were never listening at all. A good converser stays on the subject.

CHAPTER EIGHT

Speech for
the Speechless

For conversation to begin and continue, someone has to speak first. How do you get the ball rolling? What the heck do you say to a complete stranger? (And in case you're wondering, if it's about advancing your career, it is a sales proposal, not conversation.)

I've never had any trouble speaking with others. In fact I can't imagine *not* connecting in some small way with most people I encounter. The secret is that everything about my manner suggests that I am friendly and open to conversation. I walk with confidence and survey my world with a pleasant countenance. And I greet tens or even hundreds of people a day.

First, I make eye contact and smile, even if we're strangers passing on the sidewalk.

Did I lose you there? Do you think contact with strangers is a dangerous act in today's world? Go watch an old movie and you'll see that acknowledging the presence of a fellow human being was – and should be – common courtesy. Gentlemen tipped their hats to ladies and women nodded and said good day. I believe making eye contact and smiling helps me *avoid* danger. I learn a lot about a person's character in the way my look is returned – or not returned.

Schmoozability Traits

The same traits you admire in others are the ones you should develop in yourself.

Available

Schmoozers don't check caller ID and screen out those from whom they don't want anything. They're always available and keep in touch.

Compassionate

Sure, schmoozers care. They put the relationship before the business opportunity.

Dependable

Ask something of a schmoozer, and it's delivered as promised. Done right. On time.

Helpful

Schmoozers are always the first to pitch in and lend a hand when needed. They are active in charities and volunteer in professional associations.

Encouraging

Schmoozers cheer you when you're on top and console then motivate you when you're not.

Grateful

Schmoozers send thank you notes and gifts when a kindness is done them, and they do so promptly.

Curious

Schmoozers have a broad range of interests: they know a little about a lot of subjects and seek out opportunities to learn more.

And I thrive knowing I am linked on some level with everyone in the world.

Next, if the person smiles back (and they usually do), I nod and say hello or good morning. I don't pause or make any attempt at further conversation if I am passing someone on the street or in a building hallway, as that would be perceived as aggressive and perhaps frightening. I have had thousands of mini-conversations on elevators or standing in line, though.

It's a big leap from smiling at the delivery man to building a relationship that could span decades. How do you take those simple principles of common courtesy, expand them into your business and social life and create lasting bonds?

Once or twice a week, I find myself at the regular meeting of one of the many organizations with which I am associated. At a marketing association breakfast meeting, I entered the banquet hall and saw a new face standing twenty feet away. I looked him in the eye, smiled and walked up to him.

"Good morning! I'm Ty Freyvogel," I said warmly, extending my hand.

"Hello, Ty. I'm Mike Marsh," he replied.

So far, so good. (This schmoozing really isn't tough.)

Then I asked a question that will help lead me to that essential common ground we needed to have a conversation – a *meaningful* conversation. The most logical path was a question having something to do with the encounter's locale. It did not have to be profound, clever or witty.

"What have you heard about today's speaker, Mike?" I said making sure I used his name to lock it in my brain.

My question was open ended, meaning it cannot be answered by 'yes' or 'no'.

"I read his article on customer service in the newsletter. It was very interesting. But I've never heard him talk. Have you?"

"He's a pretty good speaker and very knowledgeable about customer service," I said nodding. "How much of an issue is customer service in your business?"

I answered and segued from one subject to another that – and this is important here – *he* introduced. I rarely ask a 'non sequiter' or "out of the blue" question. There's usually always a phrase or a word or a tone of voice that will help me form the next question and keep the conversation going. Remember: effective conversation is a series of comments and questions building on the prior data. You'll also note that I didn't directly ask "What's your business?" or

"What do you do?" I love my work and love to talk about it. But sometimes when someone leaps in with that question, I find something predatory about it. So I ask the question obliquely.

"Well, I'm in the carpet and drapery cleaning business dealing with commercial as well as residential customers. Customer relations are a *constant* concern," Mike said, looking concerned.

"How so?"

An amateur schmoozer (or a networker) would ask about the carpet cleaning business. But we schmooze pros know that bonds are formed through the sharing of core values, not dry facts. His thoughts on the possibly emotionally-charged issue of customer service would be of more meaning to that end.

Rolling his eyes heavenward he said, "You won't believe what my people have to put up with…" and he ranted on about the unreasonable demands customers made and how they made his life woeful. "Don't your customers drive you nuts?" he concluded.

"Customers and business are an inseparable team. Which methods have you tried to reduce customer problems and improve the morale of your staff?"

And I redirected the conversation on a constructive course. My reasons were twofold. One, I couldn't agree that customers made me nuts (they don't). But if I disagreed, I would have made his opinion "wrong", put him on the defensive and shut down our conversation before it had really begun. Two, I knew that if I allowed a conversation to revolve around negative subjects with this new schmoozee, he would forever more associate me with bad news. (And where I always sympathize with tragedy and misfortune, my dance card at the Pity Party was filled long ago.) So I rooted out the opportunity for positive action behind his negative comments.

I propelled the conversation by eliciting his thoughts, not unloading mine. Mike and I talked for more than twenty minutes that morning seven years ago. It was challenging holding this man of great inner anxiety to a proactive discourse, yet at the end, he felt confident about his ability to effect change for the better in his company.

At the next meeting, we discovered we had both been soccer stars as teenagers, and that our sons competed against each other in hockey. He gave me the name of a great sports medicine orthopedist for my bum knee.

Ever since, we have spoken monthly—sometimes about business, sometimes not— and referred business to each other. No, we're not best friends, but

I count one of the people I met through him as a close friend.

In the last few pages, I've been trying to reassure you that the progressive nature of true conversation makes connecting with total strangers easy. Perhaps you need more concrete topics for discussion.

Long ago, in a more genteel world, people were raised with a structured set of proper and improper questions. The etiquette grand dames, Amy Vanderbilt and Emily Post, set down on paper the basics of what is considered appropriate conversation in polite society.

It's dull. Real dull by today's "let it all hang out" standards. Think "weather." *"What do you think of all this rain?"*

Our forbearers understood that most initial conversation is, in fact, trivial and non-controversial. But it's trivial by design. Trivial is safe.

Just as you wouldn't play touch football in a mine field, steer very clear of subjects that have the potential to blow up in your face. Aim for areas of zero controversy. No one wants to be asked about the intimate details of their lives. And no one should really want to hear the answer. Unless you work for the National Enquirer. Anything having to do with body function is verboten, even if it is an act publicly committed by a head of state. I have no interest in talking politics or religion or, in many cases, the funding of new sports stadiums. Such subjects are often as friendly as quicksand but messier and less forgiving.

"Hot enough for you?"

I will grant that graceful conversation takes a little practice. And even those to the manor born, as they say, do sometimes err. It's been reported that Ambassador Averell Harriman froze mid bite when First Lady Jackie Kennedy leaned over at a state dinner and asked, "Have you ever seen your wife throw up?" Considering the alternatives, weather is starting to sound better and better, huh?

A step beyond weather is family. "Do you have a lot of family in town?" is a particularly suitable query around holidays. And the answer can give me great insight into my schmoozee. It teaches about spouses, children, parents, origins and leads to a wealth of other conversational topics.

As a developing schmoozer I realized how similar we all are if we have kids. So regardless of ages or schools or summer camps, there are enough common denominators between your kids and mine that we can have quite a discussion. Among the most easily accessed subjects are clothes, discipline, teachers, television, music, sports, and my personal favorite: lowering the minimum driving age to 13 so I wouldn't be a slave to car pools.

What about work?

Freud was once asked by an associate what man needed to be happy. The pioneering analyst's answer rings true today: "Why, work and love," he said. That's how important work is to us, so to compliment a person by asking about his or her work and actively listening as they speak is high praise, indeed. It's memorable praise, too.

Ty's Tips

Genuine conversation occurs when you and another establish common ground.

Again, work is vital to almost everyone and almost everyone enjoys talking about work. Some people love to complain about it and some people love to brag about it. Whichever (and there's lots of room in the middle), remember that a person's work is a large part of that person's personality.

Asking people about their work can brighten some rooms in your brain that have long been dark. The people who work in health care, for example, know tons more about the many influences in medicine than you or I. And they're often passionate about what's wrong and what's right with it. Steel, apparel, transportation, energy, education, food service ... it doesn't make much difference where a person works. That person has a lot to share with a good schmoozer.

The longer we schmooze, the more benefits fall our way. But if we take schmoozing only to a certain point and then drop it or ignore it, all the work that went into it is lost. The longer we schmooze, the easier it becomes, the less we have to think about it. Schmoozing behaviors turn into good habits.

There are situations and occasions when you will know something about the people you will meet. Maybe it's a fund raiser, a grand opening or a seminar or the first meeting of a board of trustees on which you've just been named to sit.

Don't waste an opportunity like this. If you know who will be there, take the time to learn something about them beforehand.

If you know that Ms. Jones is known not only for her prowess as a tax consultant, but is also an accomplished billiards player, learn enough about billiards to engage her in conversation.

If Ms. Donovan is best known for successful negotiating with unions, but known also for her work with battered women, make sure you're current on laws protecting women.

If Mr. Lewis is a long distance runner as well as the chief financial officer at a competitor's company, make sure you know that 10K is the length of a race, and not a dollar amount.

Knowing this information highlights another difference between a schmoozer and a networker, by the way. The networker seeks the business-only short-term gain, like a day trader. The schmoozer is interested in all that makes up an individual.

The networker says to Ms. Jones, "How do you see the current Administration's stance on taxes?" The schmoozer says, "Are there still crafts people who make custom cue sticks? And what is the preferred material for them?"

The networker asks Ms. Donovan, "Do you ever arm wrestle at the negotiating table?" A schmoozer says, "How can congress do a better job when it comes to protecting women?"

The networker says to Mr. Lewis, "I'll bet you wish you were with us, hey?" The schmoozer says, "What's the preferred style of shoe for distance running?"

Remember to end a conversation as gracefully as it began.

Ending a conversation badly can erase all the good feelings you developed in the schmooze. The usual way this happens is when you want to end the conversation before the other does. But if you're really focusing on the needs of others, and their need is to keep on talking, do you have to stand there until they get hoarse? Screaming children, barking dogs and incessant talkers *never* get hoarse.

Imagine this: your eyes are glazed, a vacant half smile is glued on your face and your eyebrows are raised to your hairline in an attempt to keep your lids from closing. Yes, someone is "oversharing". There's just no way around it: you must stop the conversation or you will surely die. Unfortunately, you haven't been able to get in a single word.

The good news is that all people are mammals and mammals, as we all know, must breathe. In fact, most of us inhale every ten seconds while speaking. It is during this gasp that the other could interject a comment.

Rabid talkers, however, don't want to leave you that window of opportunity. They take fast shallow breaths which won't sustain them for more than five seconds. Time your chatty Charlie. We are all reasonably regular respirators. If he inhales at five seconds, you inhale at four, and in that split second say, "WHAT *[stick out your hand to shake his]* a joy it's been hearing about your project. *[Keep talking while backing away.]* I look forward to hearing more about this later." *[Turn and leave.]*

Sometimes it's not so gruesome. The conversation is interesting and you do enjoy your schmoozee, but you really must go. Don't "um-hum" ever more rapidly in the hope it will hurry up the other; it just makes you seem rude. Give the other a signal that the conversation needs to come to a close. When you get the floor, recap the essence of the conversation. "Getting all those players together on that project was really a coup. When it's over, will you tell me how it all turns out?" This is one of the rare times when you want to ask a *closed* question. At the "yes" or "no" answer, stick out your hand to signal the end and say, "I look forward to it."

CHAPTER NINE

The Schmoozer Primer

Just when you thought it was safe to start schmoozing, I should warn you there are more than a few ways you can shoot yourself in the foot. (Or would that be the tongue?) They're common mistakes to make, so be alert.

Do not answer your own question. "Good to meet you, Ty. I'm Cindy," the smiling woman said when she came in to pitch ad space in her publication.

"Welcome, Cindy," I replied, pulling out her chair.

"Do you want top executives all over the country to know you and your company?" she blurted out to my back while I returned to my chair.

I tried to inhale to reply, but before I could she continued, "Of course you do. And do you want to be perceived as a leader in your field to these executives?"

My lips pursed to speak, but with glazed eyes she tore on. "Of course you do. And do you want these executives to buy from you?" A fast learner, I made no attempt to respond.

"Of course you do. And do you want to reach these executives at a low cost per thousand? Of course you do. And do you want..."

She continued on in this breathless pattern of asking and answering for the better part of ten minutes while I wondered if her train of thought had a caboose. No, I didn't buy ad space from her. And I read that her publication went belly up last year.

Do not insert your opinion in the question. Ward elbowed me as the CEO began his annual meeting presentation. "Don't you think he should be thrown out on his Ivy League keister?" he hissed.

"He's doing the best he can in these tough times, Ward," I whispered back.

"But selling off the minerals division… don't you think that was the dumbest decision?"

What I think is, any question that begins "Don't you think…" tells me *you* are not thinking. Don't try to tell the listener what he or she should think.

Allow the person to answer. Are you the type who gets itchy in the moment of silence between a question and the response? Take a few deep breaths and wait. Some people don't answer in rapid machine-gun fashion. Give them time.

Do not negate a person's response. If someone answers your question honestly and then you suggest he is stupid or wrong to think that way, you are being offensive. Whether it's as seemingly benign as saying, "I disagree" to an outright "Well, *that's* the most idiotic comment I've heard today," you will drive a rift between you and your schmoozee. (Besides, if the other person had any interest in your thoughts on this matter, you would have been asked your opinion.)

Keep it positive. "What is that hideous purple thing on that woman's head?" I overheard one woman say to another at a parent's meeting.

"That's my dear Aunt Tillie's favorite hat," said the other, turning away.

Making sport of others to initiate conversation is a big mistake. As Aunt Tillie and your mom always said, if you don't have anything nice to say about someone, you're a mean and vicious meathead. Or words to that effect.

Do not look for direct payback. I like to think that what goes around comes around, but I'm too old to believe that life is always fair. I never expect anything from the people I schmooze except basic courtesy and friendship.

Do not have a one-size-fits-all schmooze. I am very gregarious and if I am not careful, I can come on too strong for some. I look for clues, read their expressions and ratchet up or tone down my intensity, all within the confines of my unique personality.

One of the funniest scenes in "Annie Hall" is when Woody Allen says to his therapist, "We *never* have sex… maybe two or three times a week." Seconds later, Diane Keaton says to hers, "We *always* have sex… maybe two or three times a week." The point is that regular contact to one can be considered a rude annoyance to another. Adjust your schmooze to suit the schmoozee.

Be visible. This means more than just getting out of your office. The idea here is to grease the way by creating a presence. You want people who meet you for the first time to feel they've *already* met you because they've seen or heard about you.

Establish yourself as an expert in your field. Speak out on important issues. Get interviewed as a spokesman for your business or social club. Doing something to attract media attention works wonders. Something legal is best.

Be a multi-schmoozer. Schmoozers know that for the strongest bond, more than one facet of a schmoozee's life must be reached. Remember, schmoozers are not networkers, only interested in someone's profession and their own career building. The only goal of schmoozers is to connect with another in many areas which may lead to advancements in career, personal relationships intellectual knowledge… or may lead to nothing at all. Just as people are multi-dimensional, so must our approach to schmoozing. Adding children, hobbies, or sports connections to a strictly business connection, for example, gives the relationship a life that can endure even if one area of connection dissolves.

Be the driver of the bus, not just a rider. No, this doesn't mean becoming Ralph Kramden. What it means is that if you are a member of an organization, whether it's business, social or civic, take on a leadership role. Chair a committee. Start a task force. The bigger role you play, the more people you will know and the more known you will be.

Be eager to connect others. Schmoozers know it's counter-productive to schmoozing to horde all the people. So link schmoozees to each other. Their Schmooze Zone will grow and so will yours.

Be bold. It's called chutzpa. Some of you have this quality, some can develop it and others should just pass by this paragraph. Bold schmoozers schmooze anyone, from the head of the Chamber of Commerce to the head of the country. They know the worst anyone can say is "go away". So the bold do not fear schmoozing anyone, with the possible exception of ex-wives.

Memory is important, but I forgot why.

I used to lunch regularly with a retired salesman. He and I talked at length about customer service and client relations and every other subject that relates to sales. Invariably, he would be recognized by one or more people in the restaurant and engage in some very pleasant small talk. This happened regardless of the restaurant or the location. North, south, east or west of the city and in every place within city limits.

IT'S ANOTHER JOHN DOE, SARGE. I CALLED ALL 1,903 NAMES IN HIS PALM, BUT NO ONE KNOWS HIM!

I asked him once about it. "Bill," I said, "how do you know so many people?" I was especially curious because he sold chemical compounds, not the sort of product that has lots and lots of customers. His answer made me think. He said, "Well, I'm old." But he wasn't old. He was in his late sixties and in great shape. What he didn't want to do in front of me was brag. But he didn't have to brag. The many people who stopped at our tables over the years, who smiled broadly and shook Bill's hand, told me everything I needed to know.

Bill was an accomplished schmoozer. He was a natural. He was successful at schmoozing and he enjoyed his success. When an old acquaintance or friend approached the table, hand outstretched in friendship, Bill's smile was as wide as his broad shoulders and he enjoyed the adulation. Long before schmoozing had such an easily-remembered name and short list of techniques, Bill was schmoozing.

He once asked *me* about schmoozing, of all things, and I laughed. I told him I was learning whenever I was with him. I considered him to be a master. He belonged to two fraternal associations, was a volunteer with one of the arts organizations. As his four kids were growing up and getting involved in school projects, Bill and his wife, Rita, were always there. And Bill rarely forgot a name or a personal observation. He once asked an old friend who had come up to us as we left a restaurant, "How'd the llama farm do?" As it turned out, the gentleman was very successful with it and sold it two years ago. Later, as Bill and I walked down the street, I asked him how he managed to remember the man had a llama farm. Bill looked at me like a teacher looks at a helpless student and he said, "How could I not remember a llama farm?"

Perhaps we'd all remember a llama farm, but how will you remember all these people you'll meet schmoozing? How do you retain all this minutia? In the next chapters we'll cover organizing and making use of your data with the magic of your computer's database. But I do need to tell you that good old fashioned memory plays an important role in schmoozing. If someone slaps me on the back as I walk down the street, I can't say, "Just a minute, OK? I need to look up your data in my Palm Pilot."

Is your memory a little rusty? Do you have trouble putting a name to a face? Read a book on mnemonics. (That's a fancy name for improving your memory, but you brilliant guys knew that.) Word association and repetition help, too. You can strengthen your memory as you can strengthen a muscle.

PART FOUR

The Schmooze Zone

There is a dimension beyond that which is known to networkers. It is a dimension as vast as mankind and as timeless as friendship. It is the middle ground between intimacy and the unknown, between brilliance and stupidity, and it lies between the pit of self-absorption and the summit of altruism. This is the dimension of connections. It is an area which we call... The Schmooze Zone.

When I was a boy, *The Time Machine* was released starring Rod Taylor and Yvette Mimieux (also a star of my adolescent dreams). This popular movie created heated debate about whether time travel could ever be possible. One of the junior high school naysayers claimed that travel to the future was theoretically easy, but we could never travel to the past. If we went back in time it would alter the future so that the time traveler wouldn't exist. I listened as he explained that the time traveler didn't have to do something as obvious as preventing his parents from meeting. This pubescent pundit believed that we are so interconnected that virtually any contact the traveler had with anyone in the past would have far reaching influence on future events. I think I laughed at him as this was entirely too sophisticated a concept for me to comprehend then. But I'm not laughing now.

Has this happened to you? You're somewhere far away from home, on an airplane, in a restaurant, at a beach and talk to someone only to discover they

have a close tie to you. Maybe it's the brother of your next door neighbor,
the wife of a college friend or the uncle of the woman who watches your kids.
"Small world," you both say and shake your heads in wonder. Sometimes I
don't find out about the connection until I return and get a call from a friend
who informs me that I was talking to his cousin at a café in Rome. I'll leave the
answer to the question of why this occurs to philosophers and others more brilliant. I just want to establish that it does indeed happen. And with schmoozers,
it happens a lot. And it happens because we are all connected in some way.

A single act of schmoozing is like tossing a pebble in a calm lake. Each
ripple is created as a result of the strength of the prior. And it is these interde-
pendent rings which make up the fluid framework of your Schmooze Zone.

What is the Schmooze Zone? It is all inclusive, borderless. It is everyone
you touch and everyone they touch. It is those you connect with others.

Once you make contact with another, your Schmooze Zone reaches far
beyond your imagination. A reminder, networking is calculating and targeted
primarily to enhancing career goals. Schmoozing begins naturally without
design and flows like waves in the water to distant shores. By plan and by prov-
idence, it transcends race, gender, economics, religions, age, and politics incor-
porating all areas of your life: social, civic, personal as well as business.

CHAPTER TEN

Mapping Your Schmooze Zone

"Everyone is kneaded out of the same dough but not baked in the same oven," states a Yiddish proverb.

From Pip and the Convict, to Ishmael and Queequeg, beneficial associations turn up in the most unlikely of places. So why do so many hang out in the most *likely* places?

I know some very outgoing people. I see them all over town. You'd think they know everybody. And maybe they do. But it's everybody within their very small world. They go out every Saturday night, but they go out with the same few couples. They have lunch every day, but with the same few business associates. And they golf twice a week, but with the same few friends.

So while I fight the Battle of the Bulge with my waistline, they must learn to fight the Struggle of the Shrinking world. Many need to be constantly vigilant to shatter the glass walls that can creep up and block the flow of your Schmooze Zone. Just how do you do that?

I'll make this real easy: Schmooze everyone.

To the schmoozer newcomers, that may seem overwhelming. So let's make that a little more manageable and divide the world into four groups: confidants, friends, acquaintances and strangers. Confidants are those with whom you have an intimate relationship. They're your family and closest of friends. Next are those whom you call friends, speak with regularly but not about private matters. Acquaintances are those with whom you are cordial and speak with on a superficial or professional level. Strangers are simply that.

As you schmooze more and more, the number of people who know you or are getting to know you better increases. That happens for a purely schmoozer reason: You treat others as you would have them treat you.

Where to begin? Is one group better for schmoozing than another?

Ty's Tips

I'll make this real easy: Schmooze everyone.

CHAPTER ELEVEN

Who to Schmooze

Confidants. I can't imagine life without my closest friends and family. They make everything worthwhile.

That said I've discovered that my confidants are sometimes the poorest resource for increasing my Schmooze Zone. Not that they wouldn't introduce me to anyone they know, but after a lifetime of association, I pretty much *know* everyone they know. So I love talking to them, but if I limited my schmooze contacts to those I know best, I would have a Schmooze Point, not a Schmooze Zone.

That doesn't mean I don't schmooze them. I do. That's essential to maintain their high-ranking level of "confidants." I use my best schmoozer conversational skills with them as I do with others. And I am careful never to take them for granted.

There really should be a family sub-category here. If you come from a very big family like mine or from a family that has scattered over the years, you may have many relatives who are not really "confidants." Take advantage of that common bond you have and make an effort to strengthen those ties. With schmoozing, you could get to know them a lot better. You'll enjoy it and so will each of them.

Do they live on the far side or the near side of the Rockies? Make sure you take them to dinner when you're in the neighborhood. Do they have kids the same age as yours? Sounds like a reason for a family barbecue.

Friends. In the space between intimate confidants and casual acquaintances, fall your friends. I have been blessed to have many good friends in my Schmooze Zone. Now here's a group with overlooked schmooze potential. Why?

There's a sort of stand off between friends. On one hand, we are available to help friends any way we can. But on the other hand, we are reluctant to ask friends for help when we need it.

I saw this recently when a friend needed a ride home from the hospital. His family didn't live in town and his wife wasn't able to drive. He was hesitant or reluctant to "impose" on a friend and ask for a ride home. When I heard about it, I quickly arranged to pick him up and take him home. It may have taken an hour of my time, but I enjoyed doing it. We will both remember that ride home from the hospital for a long time.

We all have many opportunities to go out of our way to schmooze with friends. That's what it takes, going out of our way. The most obvious benefit in putting out extra effort is that as we become closer to other people, we have opportunities to schmooze with their friends and families. The best thing about friends? I always have room in my Schmooze Zone for more.

Acquaintances. "When I allow myself to think of the most business I have gotten from schmoozing," explains my friend, Lee, "topping my list has to be people I do not really consider friends, but with whom I have had a cordial and continuing relationship."

Here's the surprising news: research has shown that if it's results you're after, the most important ripples in your Schmooze Zone are from those in the category of not-particularly-close, but enduring.

Once a month for nearly thirty years Lee has spoken on the phone with a local newspaper ad salesman named Steve. "We talk for a few minutes about sports or occasionally our families," continues Lee. "He asks me if I want to place an ad. Sometimes I do but many times I do not. Even though our conversations aren't intimate, we have laughed through good times (his adoption of three children, my embarrassing no-run average on the community softball team), and lent an ear during bad (his daughter's tragic death, my bout with cancer). He has referred hundreds of thousands of dollars of business to me over the years (and I have returned that act of trust). And yet in three decades, we have only seen each other once."

Never ever underestimate the power of the casual acquaintance. I have stacks of evidence to prove that schmoozing in this circle is the most rewarding. And for most people, if schmoozing is done correctly, acquaintances make up a huge portion of their Schmooze Zone.

Yet when we get busy, this is the group that we put aside. Don't. These bonds are too valuable to let slip away. One of the challenges you'll face in keeping these acquaintances vital is that by their very nature contact is usually infrequent. But if you allow contact to be dropped for extended periods of time, you may lose them forever.

Once someone has become a close friend or a confidant, the relationship seldom tarnishes, even after losing touch for a long period of time. That's why we can call long-lost college roommates and pick up right where we left off.

You can't be so cavalier with acquaintances. While this group it is the most potent, it is also the most fragile.

So how long can you go between schmoozes? An older self-described "born salesman" says there's a rhythm about schmoozing. He believes he "senses" when a schmoozee needs to be contacted. For the rest of us with modest psychic abilities, there's a contact management program to remind us when someone needs a schmooze "fix."

While finding you have lost these precious acquaintances from lack of contact is reckless, purposely casting aside a contact as a result of your own lack of self-esteem is foolish. One of the most self-defeating mindsets is to think that since you are not close friends, your schmoozing will be considered intrusive. If you're truly being a pest, I guarantee someone will tell you!

Unknowns. How do you approach people you don't know? Believe it or not, the direct approach can sometimes be the best.

"Hello, I'm Ty Freyvogel," I smile and extend my hand.

Nearly everyone is approachable. By and large. You don't want to be approached through the stall door of the men's room or standing over a four-foot putt for the club championship, but in the normal course of business, being approached is a compliment, not a burden.

Remember that the next time you see someone you deem to be unapproachable. If the situation is favorable, say at a business meeting or lecture or party or dinner where conversation is welcome, simply introduce yourself. If you don't, you have no one to blame but yourself.

Striding forward, hand outstretched and smile big and toothy often works well, but it's not the only way to approach a person. Here are a few more examples and you'll probably add to the list:

Do your homework. Have you been invited to attend a charity benefit? Ask someone in the know who else will be attending. Make an effort to learn something about as many as you can. Are the two biggest corporate sponsors that night a chemical company and a law firm? Know a little about the business of each. This research will benefit you two ways: first, you will have a piece of common ground upon which to build a conversation and second, because you know what to say, your confidence level will increase.

I've never understood people who only go to parties where they know everyone. I enjoy my friends, but I welcome the chance to be able to schmooze a roomful of new faces. I don't view unknowns as strangers. To me, unknowns are opportunities.

Every new person I meet is another addition to my thriving Schmooze Zone. And I'm careful not to exclude anyone, no matter how different from me they seem.

A wise man once told me: Opportunities always look bigger going than coming.

Cal, an erratic schmoozer, told the story of the elderly woman he met on a balloon ride. "She looked like a bag lady, with her old torn clothes," he said. "I avoided sitting next to her on the drive to the field. But then I overheard her conversation with the balloon captain." He shook his head, embarrassed at his behavior. "She was the widow of a respected county judge. I recognized her last name. For years, I had been trying to get in the door at companies run by her adult children. She knew more about local business than I did. She also knew more about balloon rides, which is why when we landed in a field of cow manure she was the only one wearing old clothes and I was left picking cow chips out of my Gucci's."

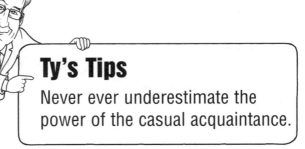

Ty's Tips
Never ever underestimate the power of the casual acquaintance.

Schmoozing at work. How can you *not* schmooze those you spend the most waking hours with? How can anyone ride up and down in the same elevator with the same people fifty weeks a year and not even know each other's names? Remember that schmoozing has little to do with corporate politics and nothing to do with secret alliances.

Work includes your colleagues, your superiors, your support staff and even your competition. It also includes the person who delivers the mail, the person who shovels the snow from the sidewalk in front of the building, and the building superintendent.

Start small. If you've never been introduced, do so. (Don't assume that since you're a big cheese with the company that everyone must already know you.) Start with the known common denominator — the company — and ask what they do for it before moving on to non-work questions. It's often surprising to learn what they do and what they enjoy when they're not at work. And you'll smile when you see how eager most people are when someone shows interest in them.

Schmoozing from the past. If schmoozing is about conversation, and conversation requires common ground, you'll find lots of schmoozees from your past.

Old school chums are a great resource. Pull out those yearbooks, go to the reunions and reconnect with your classmates. Just drop them a note or pick up the phone. "Do you remember the time when you...?" And don't limit yourself to those with whom you were closest. The passing of time is a great equalizer.

Ted hadn't been back to his hometown or had any contact with anyone in it since he graduated from high school *fifty* years ago. When he got the reunion announcement, he dusted off his yearbooks and wrote letters to several of his classmates reminiscing about the old days. Every single one wrote back, delighted that he thought of them. At the reunion, he volunteered to produce a semi-annual newsletter. That was 12 years ago. He has friends all over the country now and open invitations to visit. (You're never too old to schmooze!)

What about the people at the companies where you worked in the past? I'm amazed at how many adopt a "with us or agin us" attitude, leave a job and never look back. Is the company in the news? Call or drop a note of congratulations. People hop from job to job much more than ever before. *You* may hop from job to job. So maintaining these professional contacts benefit all.

Schmoozing across barriers. Humankind's tendency to erect fences to separate those they perceive as different is utterly counterproductive to schmoozing. This ain't networking: banish the mindset of seeking out those connections with the most lucrative payoffs. Whether someone is or isn't of the same age, race, gender, religion or socioeconomic status is of no importance to the schmoozer. If you limit your schmoozing to those who are exactly like you, you'll never learn anything new and might as well save yourself the effort.

It doesn't necessarily follow some people's logic. Some would guess that schmoozing a car attendant, for example, is not going to result even indirectly in more business and is therefore pointless. And yet on more than one occasion, I would have been late for a prospective client meeting had a car attendant not made an extra effort to bring my car down quickly. But is that the reason I talk to car a attendant? Absolutely not. We truly enjoy learning about each other.

I think women understand this. I've always suspected that they are more willing to share, while men hoard information like chips that might be needed for a future poker game. I hesitate to stereotype, but I have found that women generally have a more diverse world of schmoozees than men.

CHAPTER TWELVE

Schmoozing Unschmoozables

You know the type.

As an ice breaker, you say something like, "Hey, that Steelers game last night... wow!"

And he says, "What do you mean?"

"Well, that was *some game!*"

"What do you mean 'that was some game'?"

"It was such a heart stopper when they won it in the last two seconds."

Silence.

"Why won't you answer me?"

"Answer what?" he asks, mystified.

Why is it that you toss a ball of conversation to some people and they make no attempt to hit it back? Trying to engage these people can be excruciatingly painful. They neither answer your questions nor ask a question of you.

To most of us, a statement, particularly one about a favorite sports team, is cause to respond. ("Hey, that Steelers game last night... wow!" "You're tellin' me? I thought I'd fall out of my chair!" and the schmoozerama takes off.) But there are those who never learned Conversation 101, those who do not know how to be forthcoming. Even a direct question will result in a monosyllabic response of "yes" or "no", or just a slight nod.

True schmoozers don't need to be asked a direct question to keep the conversation going. Most of the seemingly unschmoozables do. And even that may not produce the desired result.

"Should we order in from Leo's Deli or SushiRock?" Ron asked Todd.

Todd continued to work on the inventory report.

Thinking he must not have heard, Ron cleared his throat and said, "Leo's Deli or SushiRock? Which will it be?"

No response.

"TODD!" Ron barked, "Can't you hear me?"

"Of course I can *hear* you," Todd looked puzzled, "but since I don't care where the food comes from, I didn't think I needed to answer."

As odd as an answer like this is to a schmoozer, keep in mind that there is a type of logic to it. Unschmoozeables tend to be very linear and literal folks. Nuance and subtleties of language are lost on them.

Joan told me of the time she made a radiant entrance at a formal event. When "My, don't you look beautiful" wasn't forthcoming from her date, she primed the pump with, "My, don't you look handsome in your tux."

Silence.

They walked up a flight of stairs. She started to feel a little less radiant.

Silence.

"Well?" she blurted out, feeling suddenly insecure. "How do I look?"

Baffled, her date's mouth opened and closed like a limpet before he stammered, "You...you look like Joan."

An important point to note in all of the examples above — and all actually occurred to people I know well — is that the unschmoozeable is as perplexed by your behavior as you are by his. Years ago a friend told me his wife had left him because she said he didn't love her the way she needed to be loved. It took a while for me to understand that love and schmoozing, like beauty, is in the eye of the beholder. You need to adapt your schmooze to fit the schmoozee.

Jimmy Dean said, "I can't change the direction of the wind but I can always adjust my sails to reach my destination." When attempting to schmooze an unschmoozeable, you can extend your conversation by always asking a direct, *open ended* question. Offering up a vague question with a possible "yes" or "no" response is a recipe for failure. If you want to hear more than a grunt from people like these, keep questions as broad as possible. You can further compel the unschmoozeable to answer by making and holding eye contact.

THE SCHMOOZENATOR

Have you tried that and still had limited success? Here are a few of the reasons why some seem unschmoozable and what you can do about it.

The person didn't hear you. This happens more often that you might think. We baby boomers are aging – and not always gleefully. Maybe it was the result of all the artillery in basic training years ago, maybe it was the result of cranking up the Rolling Stones on my old 8-track player or maybe it's just middle age, but I have trouble understanding some comments in a noisy environment, such as a large cocktail party or a sporting event. I'll ask someone to repeat their question three times before I give up, smile sheepishly and nod without attempting to answer. Cell phones that "cyberize" and donut-hole your speech also inhibit conversation. Solution: Look for clues. Men often turn an ear towards you, women tuck hair behind their ears, both cup their ears. Speak distinctly. Reserve important conversations for quiet areas, landlines or face-to-face meetings.

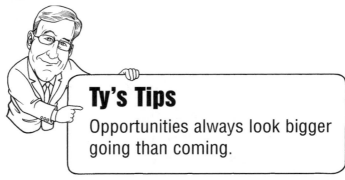

Ty's Tips
Opportunities always look bigger going than coming.

The person is distracted by external stimuli. It's a noisy world we live in. It seems that everything flashes and beeps for our attention. Companies have made a lot of money developing products that draw you in. And these products are very good at what they do. Even my car talks to me: *The door is ajar.* (The door is not a jar, idiot car computer, it's still a door.) There are times when it takes every ounce of concentration for me to stay focused without my eyes blipping to a moving marquee or a honking truck. Solution: anything more than a wave and a "howaru?" requires a peaceful venue.

The person is distracted by internal thoughts. We've all had times when we're preoccupied. Job stress, sick children, taxes, world conflict and other turmoil can create an impenetrable mental barrier. Solution: Schmoozing is about them, not you. So the only possible topic up for discussion is the one that is foremost in their thoughts.

The person is afraid. Those with low self-esteem can be paralyzed by self-consciousness and the fear that you will judge them. If this is your first meeting, they may be uneasy with strangers. Solution: choose non-threatening safe topics, such as the weather.

The person doesn't like you. Hey, it happens. Sometimes you know why, sometimes you can find out why and make amends and sometimes you just have to let that person go. Despite my best schmoozing ways, Lisa, a woman at the gym, always gave me the cold shoulder. I once asked her if I had done something to offend her but she said a terse "no" and walked away. A year later I discovered I was the spitting image of her detested ex-husband. Solution: Atone if you know you've made an offense. But draw the line at plastic surgery to appease Lisa.

The person is overwhelmed by you. There's a reason why some think schmoozers are loud and obnoxious. Some schmoozers are. If someone recoils from you, you are too close and/or too loud. Solution: Back off and tone it down as much as you can within the parameters of your personality.

The person is a weirdo. (I thought of using the term "personality challenged" or another morsel of psychobabble, but I'm a businessman, not a psychologist.) Some people just will not — cannot — carry on a conversation. I speak here of the ones who find nothing wrong in this inability, who have no desire to overcome it, and will not learn to schmooze no matter how hard you try. Many can be quite intellectually skilled and may do well in a structured business environment. Just don't expect them to be a lively addition to your St. Patrick's Day party (they probably wouldn't come anyway). The good news is that I've encountered darn few of these weirdos in my lifetime of schmoozing. Solution: Admit defeat and go schmooze some of the other six billion people on this planet.

Sometimes you get the bear; sometimes the bear gets you. So there will be instances where your charm, wit and grace fail to engage or interest someone you'd like to meet. Please don't take this personally. In fact, such rejections rarely have anything to do with the schmoozer. Want proof? Just schmooze the next person in your sights and you'll find a completely different reaction.

And we have to be aware that schmoozing, for its myriad joys, is not heaven. There are times and there are people and there are situations that can't be influenced by schmoozing. Schmoozing teaches us to understand the value of resiliency, of getting up, dusting off our skirts or trousers, and assessing the situation. Setbacks don't mean schmoozing doesn't work; setbacks mean humans are in charge and humans are prone to misdeeds, failures and unforgivable behavior. And in most cases, the virtues of schmoozing do arrive, just like the cavalry.

Power Schmoozing

1. Never pass on an opportunity to meet new people.

2. Focus on groups you enjoy.

3. Target professional groups with "automatic" connections.

4. Make an effort to schmooze older and more experienced people.

5. Remember personal information.

6. Stay in touch.

PART FIVE

Schmoozercizes

Nothing worth having ever comes easy, I remind myself as I huff and puff on the treadmill. Keeping my weight down is not always a piece of cake for me, but I work hard at it and enjoy the results. Exercise is simply an essential step for me to be successfully healthy.

Mastering schmoozer-ology may not come easy to you, either. Managing and utilizing your vast and growing list of schmoozees will require a little effort on your part. But Schmoozercises are an essential step to be a successful schmoozer.

Be patient with yourself, but be persistent as you learn the schmoozercises. Schmoozing, like breathing, is for the long haul. The relationships created and maintained by great schmoozers have little to do with the here and now, but a great deal to do with the future, both near and far.

The persistent schmoozer understands the value of restraint, but also understands that opportunity knocks only once, and sometimes knocks softly. The persistent schmoozer is quick to open the door.

And remember all days are good days to schmooze. Don't be a slacker. If you're feeling a little blue, schmoozing will lift you. I know of a woman with an internationally-known commercial art business. She also has nine children. "I tell my staff the same thing I tell my children," she relates, "Like the United

States and China during the Cold War, I do not recognize your right to have a 'bad' day. It's a useless exercise in self-pity to become egocentric and thoughtless towards others because you say you're having a bad day."

Ty's Tips

Your job as a schmoozer is to make each schmoozee feel he or she is the shiniest pebble on your beach.

CHAPTER THIRTEEN

Schmooze Management

Keeping up and current with an expanding circle calls for one of mankind's oldest and best tools: The List. Schmoozers need lists because, by and large, schmoozers know more people than non-schmoozers. Lots more. It will probably surprise you to learn how many people you know.

In pre-computer days, my father-in-law used 3 x 5 index cards. Unlike the ledger system used by my grandfather to record contacts, cards could be rearranged, deleted and added to without crossing out entries. Many people had two or three cards, each filed under a different category. It was a complex system. My father-in-law's cards soon outgrew the flip topped grey metal storage box and progressed to a system of six miniature card-sized file drawers.

But he also had something very precious and now very rare: a secretary skilled at organization and communication. Unfortunately, in the new millennium, most of us are on our own to manage our list of schmoozees. Fortunately, technology has given us a hand.

I'm told I have a great memory for people and detail. Maybe so, but I couldn't be as successful a schmoozer as I am today without my computer's contact management software.I do care very deeply for others. I also have seven children, run several companies and travel extensively as a public speaker. So sometimes my intentions are nobler than my ability to follow up. That's why I depend on my contact management program and my PDA. If I run into Dave and he tells me his daughter is ill, does it make me less of a friend if, instead of relying on my memory, I set my computer to remind me to check in on him three days later?

I created my first database in the 70s and at one time or another I've used them all: Outlook, ACT!, Goldmine, Sales Logix, Maximizer. I don't know of anyone in business today who could survive without one. But unless you're in the type of business where you sit in front of a computer all day, many of your entries will be first entered in your Palm Pilot or other PDA.

What this software does that index cards never could is organize contacts by multiple areas of my choosing, remind me of actions to take and actually generate regular schmoozing letters, print them out and have them waiting to be signed. One of the features I especially like is that it notifies me if I haven't contacted someone in, say, six months.

A critic tells me he just isn't organized and doesn't want to spend the sort of time on schmoozing that I do. I'm not organized; my computer is. And taking care of schmooze business rarely takes more than a few minutes each day.

As with any new software, there is a bit of a rough time when you are learning how the program works and all it can do. I know many executives who barely skim the surface of the functions of their contact programs. Then they get so far behind in entering data that they give up trying to stay current. The biggest hurdle is training yourself to get in the habit of using it religiously. But before you can use it, you need to collect the data to input.

When I first meet someone, business cards are usually exchanged. The back of the card is blank. For a little while, that is. As soon as I can, I jot down a few notes about the person I just met, and then slip it back into an envelope in my pocket.

What do I note? Obviously any task that I've been requested to make is at the top of the card: "send pricing" or "call for appointment". I also note the topics discussed: "World Series" or "staffing concerns". If the person has asked me to do something for him or her, I may make my notes in front of them. Anything else I save for a private moment. With every person you meet there will be some singular quality or experience that should be noted. Maybe it's: "Went to military academy/West Point," or "Little League coach," or "Races

MG Midgets." If there is something distinctive about his or her appearance, I jot that down, too: "red hair" or "very tall".

There's not a lot of room on the back of a business card and with office phones, private lines, home numbers, cell phones, faxes, business/personal e-addresses, web sites, some have resorted to imprinting the back of the card as well. If I need more room, I use those little sticky notes. And I've learned to write very small and in a sort of shorthand unique to me.

I've also learned not ever to write something on a business card that would embarrass me or the other person. I once had the bad sense to write a highly noticeable — and highly personal — physical characteristic on the back of a woman's card. A few minutes later I pulled a business card out of my pocket and hers tumbled to the floor with my comment for all to see. (And once I wrote a note on the back of my own card to buy myself new socks and under-wear. I have no idea to whom I accidentally handed *that* card.)

Every day without fail, I take a few minutes to empty my pocket's enve-lope of the day's accumulated cards and enter the information in my database. I have a nifty gadget that scans business cards. These are only about 70% accu-rate as a reader, but do save me a little typing time. Of course, I have to retype any hand written information, too. At the same time, I synchronize my PDA. This type of routine, like brushing my teeth, is what works for me.

Others like to swoop in on it every week or ten days. My cousin Hoddy Hanna uses legal tablets. He must fill a tablet every day. Another schmoozer has a big pasta bowl in his home office and into it he tosses bits of notebook paper filled with what he calls 'schmooze news.' Newspaper clips go in there, too, along with any odd idea or thought that might work for someone on his list. Every Monday he sorts it all out, adds or takes away from his list and then is able to see some of the action he'll want to take in the upcoming week. But I simply meet too many people to only tend my schmooze list once a week.

When I first started building the database back in the era of "networking", I divided the list into two parts: business and social. But not anymore. A few years ago I discovered it was impossible to classify most names. In time, all business ended up on the social list and social names turned up on the business lists. It's just the nature of schmoozing.

If it was just a list of names and addresses, my schmoozer list would be of little value. What makes a list sing is the incidentals I enter in the contact man-agement program's fields. I list where and under what circumstances we met, and distinguishing characteristics (a handlebar moustache always gets my attention; so do bow ties.) Spouses, children, interests, it all goes in. I once met a student from Arizona State University and while he had no card, I took a few notes after meeting him. I jotted down, 'very serious about golf,' and sent him many golf articles.

Some people are very, very exact with it and the data fields are numerous. Others like to keep it general and don't bother with the details. But it's the details that really count.

A funny thing happens when I enter all this information in my computer so I don't have to store it in my brain: I remember more of it!

Another delightful development is the life your list takes on. As time passes, you'll find the members on the list come to you, as often as you go to them. When that first started happening to me, it made me think of cruise control, of setting a comfortable speed and allowing the list to do what it's supposed to do. You'll know the list is on cruise control when a member of the list calls to ask for an opinion, a judgment, a professional assessment or for advice.

Have you ever sat around with a bunch of people and had someone boast of how many names they had in their Palm or Rolodex? Bradley used to work into many a conversation how he had to keep adding expensive memory to his PDA so it could hold the 7,100 names and addresses he claimed to have. "How," I would ask, "can you possibly know that many people? And why," I'd continue, "do you need to have this data with you at all times?"

I have no idea how many names are on my schmooze list. Quantity is not important. What I do know is that every one on my list knows me and I know them. Each one is a *quality* contact.

My schmooze list is confidential and to be used only for my own schmoozing purpose. I have some pretty impressive names on my schmooze list. Over the years, some have asked me for the private numbers of so and so, but I never give those out without the permission of the schmoozee. The fact that I might know someone should never be a source for bragging, but only a source for schmoozing. No great schmoozer was ever a name-dropper. No great name-dropper was ever a schmoozer.

I strive to keep my list current. It does no good and a great deal of harm to ask a member of the list to give your best regards to her delightful husband Frank only to learn that Frank ran off with the nineteen year old babysitter two years prior.

Sometimes people's feelings get hurt a little when someone mispronounces or misspells their name. So I take the time to check the spelling and make myself pronunciation clues for those on my list. The street numbers, telephone numbers, zip codes and e-mail addresses have also been checked and then checked again.

A friend of the family owns a small manufacturing company. Do you know how she refers to her list of schmoozees? She says it's her, 'sourdough starter,' the living bread dough that is the basis for one of the world's great and healthy breads. "I take care of it," she says, "and it takes care of me."

But in the end, a list is a list is a list. Making a list do what a list can do, now there's the challenge.

The list is like paving stones or bridge materials. On its own, it has little value. But when used to create paths or bridges to other people and other opportunities, it becomes priceless.

As a schmoozer, you've met people, focused on them, learned about their joys and challenges, and then remembered and recorded this information in your schmoozer list. So now what?

CHAPTER FOURTEEN

Tools of the Schmooze

All this technology is a great thing, huh? You have a slick, up-to-date list of schmoozees and a software program that will remind you when to take action. What it can't tell you is *what* action to take. That requires you. If you forget to program your computer to remind you to send a condolence note to someone the next day, or perhaps worse, send that person a condolence *e-mail* instead of a hand written note, your schmoozing efforts will fail no matter how sophisticated your contact management program. I have learned that artificial intelligence is no match for natural stupidity.

Truly effective schmoozing requires a medley of skills. Face to face schmoozing is only one piece of the schmoozer pie. Your job as a schmoozer is to make each schmoozee feel he or she is the shiniest pebble on your beach. Every time you make use of the data that you've learned, it will say to the schmoozee, "You are special enough for me to remember this."

You may have a salesman who is fascinated with the Old West. You may work with an administrative aide dedicated to the environment. Almost without thinking, you can come up with ways to acknowledge them, can't you?

Maybe you'll clip a magazine piece you saw on the death of Wild Bill

Ty's Schmoozercises

Every day...

1. I use my PDA to enter thank you notes to be written, congratulatory notes to be sent, favors to do, calls to make, or other schmoozing tasks.

2. I write notes on the back of business cards about requests for action, topics discussed, appearance.

Every afternoon...

1. I use a card reader to scan business card data into my computer.

2. I transcribe all handwritten info from the back of the card into different fields.

3. I sync the day's data from my PDA with my computer.

4. If I promised to do something, I cue my computer to remind me what to do and when to do it.

5. If I had a meaningful conversation with the contact, I enter the gist of what was said and set the computer to remind me to send a follow up note three days later.

Every morning...

1. I send a hand written note to those:

   a. with whom I had a meaningful conversation three days earlier

   b. who have done me a favor

   c. needing congratulations

   d. needing condolence messages

2. I send cards to those with upcoming birthdays.

3. I call those with a birthday today.

4. If I find an interesting article, I send a copy to those with similar interests as noted in my database.

Hickok (it was Broken-Nose Jack McCall who killed him, by the way) and send it to your salesman. You might ask your administrative aide how the company can reduce waste.

And with each action, you make them feel special. You make them feel as if their lives and the things they find important, are worthy to you as well.

If you're trying to make someone feel special, nuance matters. And of all the methods of staying in touch with others, something delivered by the post office has all the elements. I know: in today's speed of light world, a letter seems so painfully slow. By the time it arrives, you may already have seen the addressee in person several times. But mail isn't about being speedy and efficient, but being mannerly and special.

Mail is tangible, has permanence and is more meaningful because it clearly takes more effort to send. It is essential for thank you notes, condolence letters and everything in between. It is used even if you have already called on the phone with an immediate ebullient "thanks!" You must send a condolence letter even if you spent days supporting a grieving friend. Letter writing is indispensable.

Preprinted greeting cards are not synonymous with letters or notes, in my book. I do make an exception for birthday cards. Sometimes. And occasionally I'll see a funny card that cracks me up and I'll send it off to a friend. But for anything special — and my intent is always to make the schmoozee feel special — nothing can replace putting pen to paper.

Yes, it does take a little more time than signing your name on a preprinted card or sending an e-mail or calling on the phone, but the impact is worth it. And trust me on this, the more notes you write, the easier and faster it will become.

I recommend you invest in tasteful stationery. A personal note just doesn't "fit" with corporate letterhead. I love personal stationery; it allows me to add a special touch. I carry it with me to dash off notes between appointments or while waiting in the car for one of my kids. (Stationery makes a thoughtful gift to celebrate a college graduation, an engagement, a new home or a retirement, too.)

If you struggle with *what* to write, simply write what you would say out loud to the person if he or she were standing next to you. Better to send a heartfelt note with poor grammar than not to send a note at all. If you really feel like a blockhead, pick up a copy of Emily Post's or Amy Vanderbilt's etiquette books. Each has a few suggestions for letters about "life's transitions".

I send personal notes out every day. In the morning, my computer reminds me to send follow up notes to those with whom I've had a meaningful conversation three days prior. My verbiage is simple, "Great meeting a fellow hockey fan!" for example, and I enclose my photo business card. Yes, you read that right. A *photo* business card.

You may think having your photo on your business card is a little cheesy, but it's been one of the most effective schmoozer tactics I have used. After all, the original purpose of a business card is as a form of introduction. And what better way of re-introduction via the postal service, than with a picture of yourself as a memory refresher?

I do not add meaningless fluff to my initial note, such as "Let's have lunch soon!" And I don't force the relationship with a new schmoozee, by the way. There's plenty of time and lots of opportunities to further develop the relationship. What I want to guard against is appearing phony, or as one of my more acerbic associates likes to say, 'Don't be a networker.' Unless there is a reason for it, I don't suggest a further meeting at this juncture.

Let's revisit "Manners 101". My mother taught me to always say "thank you". She also told me I would be surprised at the number of people who failed to say that. So when you make the effort to say 'thanks,' you make an impression.

I always write thank you notes to people who have been kind or thoughtful or generous to me. Once you get in the habit, it's a most pleasant task. I read that no matter how late she came home or how much she had drunk or how tired she was or in which country she found herself, the late Princess Diana always — *always* — wrote her day's thank you notes before going to sleep. Let's face it, not everyone is going to make the effort. When you do, it will have big meaning to your schmoozee.

My computer also tells me when someone on my schmooze list is having a birthday, anniversary or other milestone. My recognition of that event lets my schmoozee know that they are special to me.

Many events cannot be pre-programmed and you'll just have to keep your ear out. It's vital that you keep up with the news about people on your schmooze list. In fact, the best schmoozers seem to be up on the latest news through their circle of schmoozees. Major achievements, promotions, honors, the accomplishments of the contact's children: all are fodder for a schmooze note. If someone on your list is mentioned in the news media, a note is always welcome. (If the news story is negative, the note is even more welcome.)

This brings us to the thorny issue of how to handle it when something bad happens to your schmoozee. Significant bad news always requires a written note, and frequently in conjunction with a phone call. The trick with writing this kind of letter is to try to focus on the positive angle and not merely restate the negative event. And there is always a positive side, even though it may not be readily apparent. When I send a condolence letter, for example, I write about what joy that person had brought to the lives of others and what a difference they had made in my life. So while you don't want to ignore the elephant in the living room, there's no need to spotlight it.

Recently I opened the local paper to see that the son of a woman I used to know had been arrested for theft in the neighborhood. I was shocked. You can imagine what a scandal this was in the small suburb. And as a parent, I imagined this sweet woman asking herself, "What did I do wrong?" Even though it had been more than twenty years since we had last spoken, I wrote her a letter telling her how I remembered the day she adopted her then eight-year-old son and how her good mothering skills had impressed me. I reaffirmed her shaken belief in herself. I did not mention her son's arrest.

Another time, an oncologist was lambasted as being uncaring in a newspaper series on the final days of a cancer victim. I dashed off a note to this doctor telling her how much comfort she had been to an ill relative. Again, I did not mention the negative newspaper article.

The telephone. Most schmoozing contact, if not in person, is on the telephone. I love the telephone, which may be why one of my businesses is a telecommunications company. With the advent of cell phones, most of us are "wired" 24/7. I certainly am and make brief "hi-how-are-you" schmoozing calls in the car.

Are many of your attempts at telephone schmoozing thwarted by voice mail? I schmooze almost as well on voice mail as I do when my schmoozee answers the phone. Because voice mail is so expected, I'm prepared with my message before I dial the number. Just in case.

I have my computer set to "ping" me when I haven't had contact with someone on my list in a certain period of time. Depending on the schmoozee, I have some set for three months, some for six and others for nine. All it takes to keep in touch is a quick call and an easy opening line of, "I was just thinking of the time we…" I use that frequently with people I haven't spoken with in a while. "I was just thinking of the time we heard that financial analyst speak. Is your portfolio doing any better than mine?" "I was just thinking of the time we had that conversation about our high school soccer injuries. How has your ankle been behaving?"

TODAY'S A GREAT DAY TO SCHMOOZE!

I have called people after years have passed and begun, "I was just thinking of the time we worked on that big merger that almost bankrupted us" or "I was just thinking of the time we won that big game in college" or "I was just thinking of the time we…" Try it. Reconnect with a memory shared by the two of you. And don't expect anything for it except the joy it brings you both.

E-mail. Few methods of communication have been as accessible, as inexpensive or as ubiquitous as e-mail. It needs no administrative aide or secretary to work well; e-mail is truly do-it-yourself. Few methods of communication are as fast. It's a close second to talking. And there are no long distance fees.

My favorite use of e-mails as a schmoozing tactic is the "just checking in" note or similar correspondence that does not call for a reply. It is also handy for anything I want to send to more than one person.

If I encounter an article that is intriguing, particularly from an obscure source, I pass it on to those with similar interests. (The best schmoozers, I know don't send clips from the local press, but only from specialty publications or national or international publications.) Because I list interests and hobbies in my contact's data, I can quickly send it along to those it might apply to with a note that says, 'Thought you'd be interested.' I don't over do this, rarely forward jokes and never send on chain e-mails. I also put everyone's e-address in the BCC field.

Perhaps e-mail's best virtue is its unobtrusiveness. When you send an e-mail, you're not waking anyone with a ring, you're not insisting someone listen and respond, and you're not expecting (and so you're not waiting for) a response.

It is in this impersonal nature of e-mails that schmoozer traps can lay. One of the reasons some prefer e-mail to a phone conversation is that they feel they don't have to "waste time" with pleasantries. I have never answered the phone, said hello, and had a voice bark, "Send me the Cooper report" and heard the phone slammed down. Yet my inbox is filled with statements just as abrupt.

I believe that e-mail is written correspondence and as such, demands a salutation and a closing signature. Yes, I know the recipient's name appears in the "To" field and your name appears in the "From" field. But think of that as the envelope. The letter itself still must have the traditional "Dear" and "Cordially".

Furthermore, somewhere along the line people have decided that the basic rules of grammar do not apply to e-mail. This is not true. Blocks of stream of consciousness drivel without benefit of punctuation are a recipe for misinterpretation. And if you don't care about that, consider this: Poor writing skills make you seem stupid.

Faxes. Just to make sure we cover all the methods of schmoozing without face-to-face contact, let's talk about facsimile machines. Hmmm, let's see. Faxes are muddy, difficult to read and arrogantly require the recipient to go into hock to pay for the imaging film cartridges. Faxes are for documents, not schmoozing. One day soon they'll go the way of that smelly, equally-illegible blue mimeograph paper from grade school.

Remember, schmoozing is not trading invitations every weekend for dinner. It is the smooth and comfortable business of staying current and maintaining relationships. And it gets easier and easier when your schmoozee looks forward to your schmooze. How do you get them begging for more?

Do favors for others. The Uber-Schmoozers seek out opportunities to do favors. I believe *quid pro quo* does exist whether the schmoozee is cognizant of it or not. When I do a favor for another it solidifies the bond. Even little things mean a lot in the world of schmoozing. The opportunities are limitless. But remember: if someone has to ask you for a favor it's just not the same. What kind of favors can you do for others?

Tickets. Because I have noted my schmoozee's interests, when I find I am unable to use my opera tickets, all I need to do is have the computer program search for "opera" and I have a list of contacts who would be thrilled to use the seats. Three calls later, I had given the tickets away and made a few good "brownie points" with a contact.

Buffalo Wings. I was going to Buffalo to give a talk, needed a hotel recommendation and called a buddy on my list who I knew used to live in upstate New York. He told me where to stay then said he missed the wonderful food from a restaurant that made the greatest buffalo wings in the world. So days later I drove back from Buffalo with several pounds of spicy chicken in the trunk. Our friendship is now as persistent as the greasy odor in my car.

Computers. When my company upgrades computer systems every two years, I call a girls high school to see if any could use the equipment we were replacing.

Referrals. I don't know whether I view referring a schmoozee to another schmoozee as a type of favor, but the schmoozee does. That's what counts.

Ball markers. The administrative assistant of a big client collects golf ball markers from clubs around the world. I always try to bring her one from my travels.

Be unique. Develop your own distinctive "signature" schmoozing action. A very wealthy and influential entrepreneur is known for giving Hermes ties and scarves to people he has invited to his office. The guests of another entrepreneur, not as wealthy or influential as the first, are greeted with the delightful smell of the homemade chocolate chip cookies she bakes before their arrival and then boxes up for them to take home. People clamor to be invited to the offices of either business owner. Two executives I know are welcomed into other's offices without hesitation. One executive I know always leaves a French fountain pen when he is a guest in someone's office. Yet another leaves a chocolate eagle. (None of these gifts are encumbered with company logos, by the way.)

CHAPTER FIFTEEN

Premeditated Schmooze

Up until now, schmoozing has been all about chance encounters and lack of goals. Schmoozing as a means to focus on others is the true message I want you to take away from this book. But I've been in business too long not to be a realist. Sometimes there's no way around it: you must perform premeditated schmooze.

I want something. Could be something big. Or small. A lead. A favor. A referral. The winning lottery number.

Time to mine the schmooze list. First, I sound the alert.

When I'm narrowing the field and winnowing out those who don't advance my cause, I frequently use e-mail for its ability to send many messages very fast.

(I sent just such a mass e-mail to my schmooze list when I needed that piece of sculpture pictured with me on the front cover. "Would anyone just happen to have...?" And as you can see, it worked.)

Who do you want to reach? Name anyone. It can be done. No one lives in a vacuum. People even reached the reclusive Howard Hughes, after being scrubbed down three times and wrapped head to toe in tissues. No one is unreachable. If they have contact with humans, they'll have contact with you.

Let's say I wanted urgently to reach Bill Gates. My first attack would be to send an e-mail to confidants and friends with the bold request, "I'm trying to reach Bill Gates. Do you know anyone who knows him?"

Surprisingly, tucked in with replies from my jokester pals of, "Why yes, we just had coffee this morning" may be, "No, but my sister's husband's college roommate is the brother of a Microsoft Executive VP." You just never know.

When I schmooze with a purpose, I'm never sneaky. That just doesn't suit me. As I contact those on my schmooze list I am always up front about what I want. All the good will my schmoozing has created would crumble rapidly if I were to tell others I was seeking out a particular individual for a charity auction, when all I really wanted was to sell them a product.

Ty's Tips

My photo is on my business card so no one ever has trouble putting my name and my face together.

There are many times when I'm not after a specific company or a specific person, but merely trolling for business. I have been known to use the tactic of asking schmoozees to help me "brainstorm opportunities" over a lunch. Most are flattered to be consulted and eager to assist. I get wonderful ideas for future endeavors and direct leads for current business.

Sometimes I use my schmooze list, not to connect with a prospect, but merely to find out information. I've learned surprising facts with schmooze research, saved myself a lot of time and avoided a lot of trouble. Once when I was contributions chair for a charity I got the word from my schmoozing sources that the wealthy woman I planned to schmooze as a benefactor had a steadfast rule against giving alms to the poor. My schmooze list sources were able to steer me to others with open checkbooks. Another time I was planning on buying into a business when the reports from my schmoozees alerted me to dangers that it would have taken my attorneys three months and many tens of thousands of dollars to discover.

In the end, though, premeditated schmoozing smells like networking so I try and keep it to a minimum. And if every time you schmooze someone it is of the "premeditated" flavor then it most assuredly *is* networking.

The Paradox of the Brilliant

- We have more degrees, but less sense, more knowledge, but less judgment, more medicine, but less wellness.

- We've been all the way to the moon and back, but have trouble crossing the street to meet a new neighbor.

- We build more computers to hold more information, to produce more copies than ever, but we communicate less and less.

- We've learned how to make a living, but not a life.

- We've added years to life, but not life to years.

- These are the times of fast foods and slow digestion, big men and small character, steep profits and shallow relationships.

PART SIX

Schmoozer Living

Hardly a day passes when you don't witness it or are a part of it. Road rage. One car has a near miss with another and horns blare, fists wave and expletives become projectiles. Or worse. And yet hidden cameras show that when people passing in opposite directions in a cross walk have a near collision, there's rarely an incident. Why the unbridled anger in a car?

It's in the eye contact… or lack thereof.

A brilliant woman I know is talented in the art of car schmooze. "Windshields and sunglasses are isolating enough, combine that with rolled-up windows and tinted glass and we might as well be traveling in space capsules." Everyday during rush hour, she has to merge her small car from one freeway into a tangled frenzy of commuters on a busy interstate. Those before and after her are in a dead stop for up to ten minutes waiting for a brief window of opportunity. She gains entry in just a few seconds.

Her secret? At the end of the ramp, she sticks her head out her open window, looks back, locks eyes with approaching drivers, smiles and then points to the lane she wants to enter. If she makes eye contact, she always receives a waved hand as permission to merge, and she usually gets a smile in return, too. It is a moment of simple non-verbal schmoozing. And schmoozing is her way of living. Even in a car.

Would she fit the ideal schmoozer template? Frankly, I don't think there is one. When I try to describe the perfect schmoozer, personality has little or nothing to do with it. There is no one personality type, as far as I can tell. Introverts as well as extroverts have been successful schmoozers.

At first I thought education played a role, because many schmoozers know so much about the world around them. Then I met a great schmoozer named Jeffery. He is 32 years old and has an IQ of 39. According to the experts, he is supposed to be barely verbal. But no one ever told that to Jeffery. So he may not read or write but he talks to everyone, delights in everything, organizes dances with the county group homes and is loved by all.

Income certainly has nothing to do with it. Neither race nor national origins play much of a role. If religion has an influence, I don't know what it is. One of the best schmoozers I know practices Buddhism and Shinto, and he told me something I should have seen myself. "Schmoozing," he said, "is not solely the American way, not solely the European way, not solely the African way, and it's not solely the Asian way. It's fundamentally the way of *all* people."

CHAPTER SIXTEEN

Schmoozing is Transforming

I can't say for sure when it first happened. All I remember is the day when it first dawned on me that I had changed. I had started the day with the intent on finishing year end reports. By late afternoon, after fielding more than 20 phone calls, the unfinished reports were still strewn across the desk. I should have been frustrated and upset. But I wasn't. In pre-schmoozer times, I might have considered all these calls unwelcome intrusions. As a schmoozer, I see surprise calls and visits as opportunities.

Schmoozing changes us and changes the way we see others. We look not for faults or weaknesses, but for virtues and strengths. What a surprise that is!

But it figures, doesn't it? A schmoozer is not auditioning to be a contestant on a game show. Just the opposite. All the changes happen without announcements or fanfare. Yet few schmoozers, upon reflection, would deny they haven't enjoyed the following changes, though the changes didn't necessarily come in the following order. And there are more benefits, but these are the ones most schmoozers report.

Self esteem changes, too. Little hints give it away. The schmoozer whose self esteem has been elevated by schmoozing looks different. He stands a little taller, smiles a little more and takes more care in dressing. He feels better about himself and therefore looks better. When he or she takes on a project, it's taken on with an air of confidence.

Ty's Tips
The first step to regaining trust is simple conversation.

And what about income? It is the one change that is always described roughly the same way: "I don't know how, but my income really did go up." Even after all the men and women who have explained it to me, I still don't know precisely why. Does schmoozing, perhaps, free the mind and allow it to make more advantageous deals? Is the mind able to produce more in the same amount of time as before? Are expensive mistakes no longer made? Beats me. This is a change I'll always study. It's fascinating that it has such a positive effect on such a high percentage of schmoozers, yet no one can really put a finger on it.

Yes, schmoozing has changed me. It even changes the way I view change. And it's a change for the better.

CHAPTER SEVENTEEN

Schmoozing Salvation

If it has the power to change people for the better, can schmoozing save the world? That's a rather tall order. I don't know, but I'd like to believe so. I do know that schmoozing can make it a safer place in which to live. And that's a pretty good start, in my book. In the not-so-long-ago "old days" when telephones were answered by human beings, the neighbor's kid pumped the gas in your car, and everybody schmoozed everybody all the time, there was less suspicion, less fear.

And then we stopped connecting.

How did this happen? As with all behavioral changes, it can be insidious; each successive snub of another becomes easier and easier. If one day you don't say hello to the new boy who bags your groceries, the next day it's simple to ignore the elderly man at the bus stop. If one day a delivery woman silently thrusts out the overnight package as you silently sign the receipt, the next day it seems natural to push your deposit to the teller and leave without speaking.

We've become shut-ins and there is an epidemic of cabin fever in the land. But the walls of our cabins are made not of wood, but of distrust. John Donne was wrong: we *are* islands.

I'm not a psychologist or sociologist or anthropologist or biologist or any other 'ist', but it doesn't take the brilliant to see that not meeting the minimum daily requirement of conversation can create an abyss of anxiety.

When many if not most businesses could be "virtual" with employees working on a computer at home, why aren't they? Do we know – deep down – that communication, particularly face-to-face communication, is indispensable? Indispensable for our businesses. Indispensable for our sanity.

CHAPTER EIGHTEEN

Make the First
Schmooze

When I was growing up if an adult spoke to me, I froze on the spot and respectfully replied, "Yes ma'am" or "Yes Sir." Now we have a second generation of children reared with a mantra of stranger danger: unknown adults are to be feared and avoided. In fact, all strangers – adults and other children – have now become suspect. These skittish children grow up to be wary adults. And the trepidation increases exponentially by generation.

Perhaps that's why no one trusts anyone anymore. It's obvious wherever you go. Ninety-nine point nine percent of consumers are honest yet retailers scream, "I don't trust you not to shoplift!" by limiting the number of garments that can be taken in a dressing room, or erecting theft sensors at every door. And each of us shouts the same statement when we cling to sociocentrism and wall out the majority of the more than six billion people on this planet.

Does barricading ourselves from the unknown make us safe? To the contrary, I believe shutting a group on the outside keeps the door to fear wide open.

My head's not in the sand. I know there are those who have committed vile, inexcusable and unspeakable acts in this world. I want to protect my family from them as much as you. But I have to identify them first. And schmoozing helps me do that. Knowing my neighbor won't eliminate evil doings, but it will eliminate my fear.

Ty's Tips

Schmoozing changes us and changes the way we see others. It even changes the way we view change. And it's a change for the better.

The first step to regaining trust is simple conversation.
Make the first schmooze.

Schmooze your neighbors. Schmooze your co-workers. Schmooze the rich. Schmooze the poor. Schmooze the elderly. Schmooze the young. Schmooze your community. Schmooze the strangers and they'll be a stranger nevermore. The more you schmooze, the safer you'll feel. Make their lives a part of yours and your fear will disappear.

You can make a difference. As Margaret Mead said, "Never believe that a few caring people can't change the world. For, indeed, that's all who ever have."

Just make the first schmooze.

Acknowledgements

I would never have had the courage to take on this bold task if not for the life-long guidance of my father, Thomas Freyvogel, Sr. He was the best of the best. I miss him every day.

I can't fail to recognize those whose rich stories made this book come alive. Thanks for letting me immortalize you.

This book would never have been possible were it not for the efforts of so many special people. My heartfelt thanks go to...

Gayle McCrystal, my agent, publisher, editor and friend. When I think about your dedication and tenacity to this project, especially when it looked impossible, I am reminded of what Winston Churchill once said at a commencement exercise, "Never, never, never, never give up." You exemplify these qualities and much more. You are an extremely gifted person. I am grateful to you.

An old friend, talented schmoozer and person I admire very much, Rocky Bleier.

The talented book designer, James Simko. He "nose" why.

Albert Einstein who said, "A person starts to live when he can live outside himself." Several years ago I was in Washington DC visiting the Viet Nam Memorial and spotted his statue across the street. I had to have my picture taken with the great American scientist. I never dreamt we would have this chance to schmooze.

All the people who schmoozed me throughout my life and sought nothing in return, and to all those who allowed me the honor of schmoozing them.

My family who is always there to lend a hand.

And to God who has a hand in all things.

Ty Freyvogel
October 2001

Ty Freyvogel

is a successful businessman, noted author and exciting speaker. This entrepreneurial dynamo thrives on the exciting challenge of owning and growing his portfolio of companies. Ty has founded or transformed more than a dozen small and million-dollar enterprises.

Long before the AT&T breakup, this visionary presaged the potential of telecommunications consulting and created Bayard Communication. In one of his most dramatic turnarounds, Ty bought a failing weight loss franchise and whipped it into a record-breaking success.

Today, Ty owns all or part of several different businesses and is an active investor in many diverse companies. He views schmoozing as part of a series of social changes that are sweeping America and the world.

As an admired public speaker and author of It's Not Your Smarts, It's Your Schmooze: How to Succeed Without Being Brilliant, and Seize the Century! Turnaround Tactics for Success, Ty travels the nation with his message of success through schmoozing and maximizing the abundance of the universe. He resides in Pennsylvania with his wife Katherine and their seven children.

Schmooze some more!

Order additional copies of
It's Not Your Smarts, It's Your Schmooze and
Seize the Century! Turnaround Tactics for Success
www.TyFreyvogel.com
(888) 346-8638

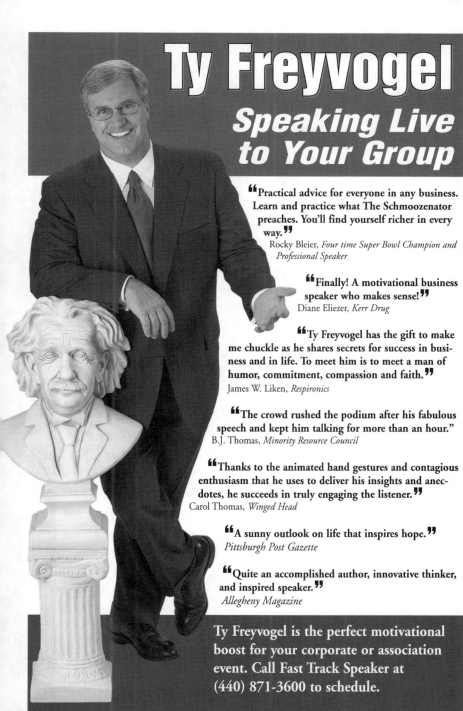